For

Vin McEhen

WINDOWS ON
A PATH TO GRACE

A GUIDEBOOK FOR
THE SPIRITUAL JOURNEY

by

CAROLINE McCUTCHEON

1ST PUBLISHED BY

Ring of Grace Publications
93 Clarendon Drive
London SW15 1AN

ISBN 0-9537194-0-5

With thanks to Barry
and to all who guided me

Typesetting by Janice Williams
Printed and bound in Great Britain by The Basingstoke Press (75) Limited
Basingstoke, Hampshire, RG24 8QW

FOREWORD

This book is a guidebook for the spiritual journey. When I was twenty-one years old I searched for a book that would explain to me what the spiritual path was about, and where it would eventually lead me. Finding no such book I started a path anyway, joining a Sufi Order and remaining there for fourteen years.

I realised through these years that the true path of my spirit was not one I could find described in any book. The most important part of my spiritual development came from learning to be honest, patient and brave. My growth in honesty eventually meant that I had to leave the order in which I had grown up. Becoming honest meant seeing through much that I had believed in, and leaving it behind. This was six years ago. I hope that this book encourages you to find your own way, and to see spiritual growth as a process that affects your everyday life in a meaningful way.

I have used the image of a domed tower with windows and a spiral staircase to illustrate the steps of a human path. Through each window a light shines that helps you find your way. This image conveys the process of gradual illumination that accompanies genuine spiritual growth, and gives an idea of the stages that many people go through, in one way or another.

The best way to read this book is to take your time; to read a chapter a day, or spread it out even more. It is a good idea to take a break in between stages in order to reflect on the material. Most of the chapters suggest practical ways in which the ideas talked about can be integrated into everyday experience. In the last section of the book detailed instructions describe how to receive the rays of grace, and how to use their blessing to heal your life.

I hope this book helps anyone who wants to know what a spiritual path is, and where it leads. I also hope that it inspires some to open the door of their heart, and step forward on a path to grace.

CAROLINE MCCUTCHEON
OCTOBER 1999

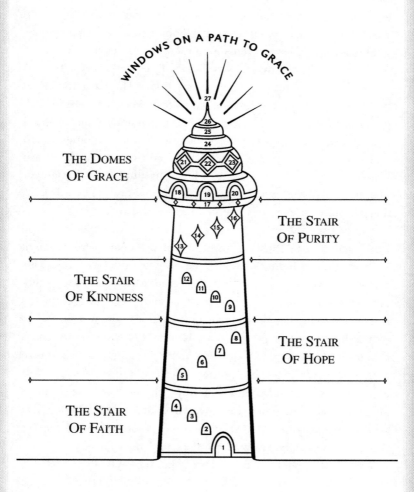

WINDOWS ON A PATH TO GRACE

THE DOMES
OF GRACE

THE STAIR
OF PURITY

THE STAIR
OF KINDNESS

THE STAIR
OF HOPE

THE STAIR
OF FAITH

CONTENTS

THE STAIR OF
FAITH

1

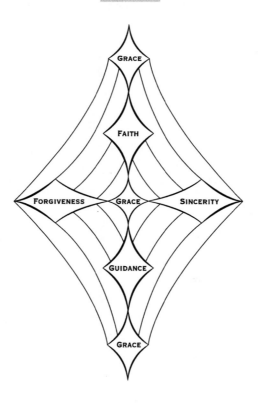

The Door of Faith
◆
The Window of Forgiveness
◆
The Window of Guidance
◆
The Window of Sincerity

THE STAIR OF FAITH

**Where the individual opens their heart to the
light of faith and finds within a path to grace**

The stair of faith is a stage in our lives when we
feel the need to find a deeper meaning to our
existence. To open the door of the heart we need
to find some faith in our capacity to love and trust.
To progress we need to learn to forgive, both
others and ourselves, as forgiveness sets us free.
Guidance helps us see the way ahead. It may come
through the medium of someone who has travelled the path before, who can help us progress. It
may come through a connection with a spirit guide.
It may involve trusting the direction of our own
inner light, rather than the guidance of an outer
teacher. The step of sincerity helps us to become
more honest, so that we can truthfully reflect our
inner light.

The light of faith, the light that lies behind the
locked door of the heart, is the first spark of our
inner light. The spiritual journey is a journey to
realise this divine spark, to uncover it and express
it fully. The windows on the way provide us with
illumination, to make this journey clearer and less
hazardous. The first step, of faith, leads to the last
step, of grace. What lies in between is an illumined
staircase that takes us home, as we find within a
path to grace.

THE DOOR OF FAITH

The door of faith lies within you, waiting to be opened. It is a door in the heart that shows you a different way to be. Until you are ready to change, you do not find this door, this point of access to an inner path. As you open the door you find a way of living through which you will grow in wisdom, strength, humility, understanding, and love. Until you are ready to begin a process of conscious inner growth, you won't see the door.

Before you find this door it may be that you lose faith in everything you have been taught to believe in and trust. Real faith does not depend on anything anyone has ever said; it is a light in the heart that brings you peace. It may be that you find faith as your world is crumbling, as you lose something that you think defines who you are. Faith can be found in a crisis. The loss of relationships, income, status, identity, all of these things can trigger a process of change in which faith is unexpectedly found. Understanding that all you hold on to can be lost, may show you something you don't need to hold on to, something that is always there.

Something that is always there is the light of your essence, the inner light that illumines your soul through its incarnations in form. It is the divine spark that lies at the centre of your being. As a human being you have the opportunity to recognise this spark within, to nurture it and let it grow. This is a light that will illumine your path, the light of your essential grace. It is this light, the light of your centre, that you catch a glimpse of through the door of faith.

THE POWER BEHIND THE UNIVERSE IS LOVING

To have faith is to know that ultimately the purpose and the power behind the universe is loving. Without this faith you cannot feel secure. Security that outlives all you can own or strive for, comes from faith. This security enables you to see more clearly. To see clearly is to see your way, to see why you are here, to understand your purpose on earth. It is hard to do this without faith.

The light of faith helps you to fear less, as you begin to love more. It helps you to feel the healing power of the universe, the creative power of love. It helps you to find your own healing power, through a way of being that is loving. Love is the true power in the universe that you discover on a path to grace. This is the power that is everlasting. You cannot find it without faith. The light of faith helps you understand your purpose on earth, your real purpose, which is to evolve. This has always been our purpose, both collectively and individually. Your divine or higher consciousness has always known your true purpose, and this is what makes your journey a process of remembering rather than painfully learning from scratch. Inside us all is the blueprint of our own divinity, no matter how hidden. We are essentially divine, and connected to all other life that is also of divine origin.

'Divine' is a word that means nothing to many people. To some it suggests an ideal, that is difficult or impossible to attain. To me the 'divine' means a feeling of unconditional love. This feeling always was and will be, and it has always been what we are in essence. That is why we feel closer to the divine when we love. We are closer to what we are, to what is lasting and real in us. Our path, our journey, is to uncover and become the unconditional love that we truly are.

FINDING THE LIGHT OF FAITH IN YOURSELF

If you doubt that the divine is love, and that this is your essence, explore what it is to feel love. Many of us were not loved enough as children to know what it feels like to be unconditionally loved; but all of us can experience what it feels like to love another unconditionally. Focus on one person in your life: it can be your mother, your child, your partner, your friend, the person who lives next door, your pet. Look at them and accept them, and see them. See them for the being they are, fragile and easily hurt, just like you. See their dreams: imagine the hidden aspirations that make their hearts sing. Forgive them their lack, their need, their thought-lessness, their defensiveness, their pain. Begin to see the beauty that is hidden within them, begin to see the potential that they possess. All of us possess great inner beauty and grace, but few of us take the time to see it in another, or in ourselves. As you take the time to see another human being, you open up a capacity for gentleness within yourself that transforms your experience.

To discover an opening to gentleness in yourself is the key to the door of faith. As you turn the key, allowing a gentler vision to inform your perception, you open the door. Once you begin to open up, a distant memory may resonate within you. This is a memory of the love that you truly are. Through seeing another with love you open up to the possibility of seeing yourself, of seeing the love that you are, that ennobles and transforms you.

As your heart opens, your journey begins. The door of faith opens as you find faith in your own capacity to love. This gives you faith in a loving universe. As you pass through the door of faith, a deeper dimension to living opens up within you. You may realise that there is more to life than material success. You may suspect that the feeling you have found holds for you a sense of fulfilment that other avenues cannot offer you. You may know nothing about spirituality at all, and this is not important. What matters is the opening of the heart, the capacity you have found to love, to hold another being in your loving sight. It doesn't matter if you have faith in nothing else, it is enough that you have faith in a new way of seeing, a way that promises a deeper understanding of yourself.

A PATH TO GRACE

Grace is our natural state, the state we are born to live in. We have forgotten how to be this way, just as we have forgotten how to see through eyes that love; but we can learn again, we can remember. We remember as we progress upon a spiritual path. Because we have forgotten much, and are used to living in forgetfulness, the path before us has many steps, and will take us many years. In truth it is just one step, the step of being loving that starts with faith and ends with grace. The reason there are so many stages to the path, is that it is hard to take this big step all at once, our evolution is a gradual process. Our first small step begins as we open the door of faith. The more able you are to open your heart, the less you need to worry about the outer trappings of any formal path of spiritual transformation. Your transformation will happen by itself if you open up to the loving power of your own heart. Within your heart is the light that will guide you home. Trust it and you will never lose your way.

THE FIRST STEP ON THE TOWER OF GRACE

As you pass through the door of faith, the lantern of your heart illumines the darkness before you. Through the gloom you see a spiral staircase winding upwards through a tall tower. Above each step is a dark window. As you walk forward and place your foot on the first stair, the window above it lights up and illumines the step below. You realise that a path to grace has always been here for you, but until you passed through the door you never knew it was there. Spiritual illumination, strength, wisdom, assistance, instruction and blessing flow to you from the illumined windows of the tower, once you have found the courage to step alone onto the first stair. Now you understand that each window is there to help you, and that as you climb the stair you will leave a path of light behind you. With relief you turn your face towards the first illumined window of the tower of grace, the window of forgiveness.

THE WINDOW OF FORGIVENESS

The light from the window of forgiveness shines on you as you step upon a path of return. The light of forgiveness helps you progress with more understanding of yourself and your history. Your journey now becomes one of recovery from pain and suffering, a journey into healing and wholeness, a journey into grace.

The light from the window of forgiveness transforms your perception, by showing you that you are not to blame for all you have suffered. This light helps you to see that you suffer most through your lack of understanding. A journey of return begins as you release the burden of misunderstanding that you have carried through your lifetimes on earth. You lift this burden as you learn to forgive.

To become more conscious involves understanding why we are here on earth, the reason for our successive incarnations. It is not necessary to remember and go through numerous past lives in order to understand this. Karma is concerned with action and reaction, the results of all our previous actions contributing to the sum total of our individual karmic load. This is the load that we begin to release through a conscious process of forgiveness.

Nobody's lifetime has been free of oppression in one form or another, and oppression causes karma. Whether we have curtailed the free will or freedom of another, or whether they have prevented us from fulfiling our potential, karma is always involved. Karmic reaction affects the one who is oppressed, as well as the oppressor, for both are locked within its chain. None of us can be free until we learn to forgive others and ourselves. In this way our future is transformed, as there is no need for us to go through the same power struggles that were our lessons up till now. We can forgive ourselves for having acted with cruelty, and for having been victimised.

To forgive yourself for having been a victim, is to free yourself from an oppressive dynamic. You are then able to realise your true identity as a loving being. Whatever happens to you in your life you cannot be a victim if you chose love. This understanding leads to strength and liberation. Nobody can rob you of your essential light, which is loving, eternal and true.

FREEDOM FROM THE VICTIM AND OPRESSOR WITHIN

By understanding and forgiving the victim and oppressor inside ourselves, we learn what our lifetimes have been seeking to teach us. There is no escape from the victim and oppressor within except through love. There is no way to avoid the same mistakes, the same patterns, the same controlling relationships except through unconditional love. Until we learn this we keep replaying the same old tune in our lifetime, and through different lifetimes, with slight variations. Until we consciously realise that in forgiveness lies our freedom, there is no way to hear the symphony of love that beckons us to leave a worn out tune. Through the note of our heart's forgiveness we begin to hear it, as we transform our future. Our existence can now spontaneously express the love that we are in essence; and the compulsion to repeat the same old tune has gone.

The same old tune that kept us in a circle of oppression, is the song of our fear and pride. Fear keeps us from forgiveness, as it locks us in a circle where the strong enslave the weak. Pride keeps us from forgiveness, as to forgive involves becoming open and vulnerable, and this you cannot do if you are proud. To take the step of forgiveness is to understand that freedom is not found through the strength of a tyrant, or the weakness of a slave. Freedom is found through a love that is strong enough to forgive.

FINDING THE LIGHT OF FORGIVENESS IN YOURSELF

If you would like to find the light of forgiveness in yourself, the following meditation may help. Find a quiet space and time, and relax your body as you release your breath. Ground yourself by sending out roots from your feet, and a taproot from the base of your spine, deep into the earth. Feel the energy of the earth holding you. Centre yourself by finding a still point in the centre of your body, as you become aware of the rhythm of your breath.

Imagine a tiny baby at your centre, fragile and easily hurt. Recognise the child within that you have denied. This is the part of you that desperately needs love, and that fears it will never receive it. This part of you has tried in many different ways to become a person that others would love, has conformed in order to be accepted, in order to receive love. To find the child within you that is desperate for unconditional love, is to find a safe place within where you can love yourself just as you are.

As you find your own needy child, open up your arms and hold them, love them just as they are, with the unconditional love that they crave. Hold your child in your arms and ask to be forgiven. Ask your child to forgive you your lack of love, your lack of care. Ask to be forgiven for all the times you ignored their pleas for gentleness, all the times you wouldn't listen. Ask for forgiveness as you give unconditional love.

Promise to hear your inner child, promise to care for them, promise to be there for them. Learning to love your inner child with unconditional love is the first step to healing the wounds of a lifetime. Learning to love your inner child, and learning to care for them, frees you from blame, and enables you to forgive both yourself and others. Until you forgive yourself for being less than kind and less than gentle, you cannot forgive other people. You will externalise your own conflicts, and hurt them as you hurt yourself. By loving and listening to your own child, and asking for their forgiveness, you make self-forgiveness possible. You heal your own wounds as you hold your own needy child. Through this deep healing you can begin to heal your life, and recover your capacity for unconditional love.

SHARING THE LIGHT OF FORGIVENESS WITH OTHERS
A second part of this meditation may be included when you are ready for it. When you have made contact with your child, have held them and cherished them, you can go on to love and forgive the child in others.

Focus on one person whom you cannot forgive. It may be your father, your mother, your sister, your child, your partner, or your old friend who betrayed you. Focus on them and see their inner child, a child like your child, fragile and easily hurt. See them fighting as you have fought, fighting to hide their pain. As you open up and receive your inner child, receive theirs also. Whatever they have done to you, whatever you have suffered, forgive them as you hold them. All of us hurt one another because we fear to be hurt. By finding the strength to heal yourself, you cease to fear the cruelty of others. By finding a path to gentleness in yourself, you find a way to disarm the most vicious, as you hold their little child.

Disarm them with forgiveness as you see them with love. Embrace their inner child, as they cease to terrify you. Hold their inner child in your arms in this meditation, as you forgive them. Let the light of forgiveness heal your life.

Those that we are closest to, are sometimes the hardest to forgive. When you feel a deep revulsion against letting go of fear and hatred towards someone, find the gentleness to love. Ceasing to resist can feel like powerlessness, but in fact it is the beginning of real power. You free your destiny as you cease to resist the pull of love. You may fear that others will trample all over your heart and leave it in ruins. Yet an open heart is the only place where you will find forgiveness and reconciliation. That which you keep most heavily guarded, is the light that now wants to shine forth as you open up and forgive. It is only through becoming vulnerable that you are able to forgive. It is only through an attitude of openness that you are able to let go of your own fear. As you release your hatred and blame, you are set free.

To trust your own growth is to trust that you can choose love and gentleness instead of hate and fear. It means taking a step towards loving yourself, your real self. You take your first step to freedom as the light of forgiveness illumines your heart.

Unless your first steps include forgiveness, your path may not help you to evolve. Without the safeguard of forgiveness, any path can be misleading. As we grow in evolutionary understanding, we grow in spiritual power. Therefore it is important that you begin a path understanding that you have a responsibility to yourself never to harm anyone else. You have a responsibility to your own child, and to the child in others. You begin by learning how to forgive. It is important to do this when you begin, so that later when you have more strength and power it is used for healing, and not for combat.

The second step on the stair is now before you; as you step upon it light streams down from a window above. This new light, which is here to help you as you climb, falls from the window of guidance.

THE WINDOW OF GUIDANCE

Having begun your path, you may feel the need for guidance. Guidance can come in many forms. Some people want a living guide, a human being whom they consider to be further along the path, someone who can take their hand. Others choose as a guide a great teacher no longer living on earth, whose path they try to follow. The written teachings of such individuals provide them with direction and assistance. Some choose to receive help from a discarnate guide, one who has been with them since before their birth in this lifetime. Such a guide can be a source of great assistance. Some people seek the guidance of their own inner light, as they follow the still small voice of the heart. You may seek direction from all of the above, at different times in your life.

Genuine spiritual guidance is a valuable means of helping you progress. However, there are dangers in accepting guidance, especially from a living guide. There is the obvious danger that you may choose a guide who cannot lead you anywhere worth going. If you feel the need for a living guide, how can you be sure that the one you find will help you? If you wish to advance through this relationship, you will have to trust your teacher, and their motives in offering to guide you.

Those who are true guides have realised their true point. They can help you find and realise your true point, the point of light that illumines the heart. A true guide may follow a spiritual path that has its roots in an ancient tradition, or they may not. But whether or not they are allied to an ancient school, a true guide will be illumined by their inner light, and it is this light that they will help you discover in yourself.

A true guide is motivated to help you find your light in order to contribute to the enlightenment of humanity as a whole. He or she is evolved enough to understand that the evolution of one is the evolution of all. Spiritual evolution has both an individual and a collective aspect. Those who have evolved sufficiently on their individual path recognise that assisting others on their journey is one way to further the collective journey, the evolution of the whole. As we are all part of this whole, none of us can be completely evolved until we all are. Thus, our spiritual path can never only include ourselves: we take the rest of creation with us, at every step.

In this way the teacher's own spiritual evolution may motivate them to guide others, and their guidance will be rooted in an understanding of the whole evolutionary process. They will guide with compassion, as this is how their inner light is outwardly expressed. Their assistance is an outward expression of their love for creation, which is in truth one body, one unified whole.

A LINK OF THE HEART

Such a guide can help you see through the illusion of separation by sharing with you the light in his or her heart, which connects to the inner light in yours. They are both essentially the same light, but the guide's light, being stronger, will feed yours. In this way a link of the heart is born, as your heart responds to a ray of its own light, coming to it through the window of an illumined guide. Because this light is graceful in essence, this link also has a graceful quality. It mirrors the relationship of grace that links the divine to creation. What this means is that the ray of light that links your heart to theirs is essentially the same as the rays of creative light that link all being to its source. For this reason when you meet someone who can guide you, you may feel a sense of connection that has nothing to do with his or her individual human personality. This heart link bypasses the personality, both theirs and yours, and forges instead a deeper connection of grace. This connection does not depend on the things that keep alive the connections we have with other people, such as mutual self-interest. It feels different from other relationships, though we may not consciously understand why. A true guide nourishes a seeker's heart, which uses this nourishment to become more illumined. All that you have to do at this stage is open up to receive.

RECOGNISING SELF-INTERESTED TEACHERS

Before you do this, be sure that your guide is trustworthy. Although prospective teachers may be accomplished in many ways, if they have not yet become human they cannot guide you home. Becoming human involves becoming unable to inflict harm on others. This happens when you lose a self-orientated perspective, and experience unity at a deep level. Because of this identification you are unable to harm any part of the whole. You become harmless, a servant of universal love. Self-interested teachers however, are not moving in this direction. They are still driven by self-centred goals. Through their teaching you may grow in occult power, but nothing that you learn will help you evolve into a compassionate human being.

Such teachers attract seekers by making an inner connection with them that is forged not through the heart's compassionate light, but through human need, the need of the personality of both guide and seeker. The need may manifest on the guide's side as a need to be respected and admired, and on the seeker's side by a need to be taken care of, directed and fed. There is no eternal connection, no link of grace. Through a link of human need, seekers may be damaged by teachers who lead them into a state of emotional dependence that does not help them to discover their inner light at all.

Sometimes a guide is unaware of what they are doing, and would not deliberately set out to mislead others. They may have been badly taught themselves, and are teaching as they were taught. However, some teachers are fully aware of what they are doing. They may have reached a point of futility in their own journey, where nothing has any meaning. With this sense of futility people may end up guiding others for all kinds of reasons, none of them compassionate. They may teach in order to gain power and influence over people, to feel important, to attract admirers, or to gather financial rewards. Their motives will be rooted in self-interest. As a seeker it is important to discriminate, to ascertain the motives of your guide, and to see where you are being led.

SAFEGUARDS WHEN CHOOSING A SPIRITUAL TEACHER

If you are in touch with your heart, you may be able to sense intuitively the inner reality of a teacher, by the way you feel in their presence. The light of compassion that shines from the heart of a true guide feels different from the energy of need generated by guides whose motives are less clear. If you cannot yet be sure of your ability to discriminate, there are a few outward criteria you can use to assess the integrity of a prospective guide.

These are:

1. Are they are honest?
2. Are they humble?
3. Are they motivated by compassion?
4. Are they using their position as a guide to exploit anyone?
5. Are they independent? Do they need you?
6. Who is behind them? Do they work for the truth, for themselves, or for an organisation?

If you meet someone who passes this assessment, his or her guidance will probably help you. However, even with a true guide there are dangers. You may become dependent on the direction, assistance and spiritual nourishment of your guide, and find it hard to make decisions for yourself. The guide may become attached to you. It can never be a completely equal relationship. This is why it can cause problems, and slow down your growth at some stage. You may have to leave a living guide in order to progress in your own way, finding your own style, and breaking free of the confines of an unequal relationship.

You may intrinsically distrust this way of learning, either because you have known untrustworthy teachers, or because you recognise that being led by a living guide is not the best way for you to progress. You may decide to seek guidance from other sources.

RECEIVING GUIDANCE FROM A SPIRITUAL TEACHER OF THE PAST
Some people seek inspiration and guidance from an individual no longer living, who was a great spiritual teacher when they were alive. Examples of two such teachers are Jesus and Buddha. Such assistance can always be trusted, provided that it comes direct from the source to your own heart, through words that they have written, or through a sense of communion between your soul and theirs. The organisations that have grown up to expound the teachings of great souls are not always trustworthy. Individuals within them may have tampered with the original message, to promote their own interests, in a way that denies the loving spirit of human equality that great teachers always stress. In addition the influence of group conditioning, of belonging to a particular group and of

being intolerant of others, can limit individual perception and prevent you opening up to the light within. Therefore although great teachers of the past can always be trusted, you need to be cautious about embracing the guidance of religious organisations which have grown up to expound their teachings.

RECEIVING GUIDANCE FROM A DISCARNATE GUIDE

Some people find assistance from a discarnate spirit guide, a guide who no longer exists in this realm, but who is available to help souls who are seeking to evolve. All of us have a personal guide, one who has been with us through our lifetime, and maybe through previous lifetimes as well. This guide knows us well, and is aware of the spiritual lessons that we need to learn in this present incarnation. They are always with us, but do not usually contact us unless we decide that we want to make a connection with them.

If you find it hard to make a connection with a guide, or hard to communicate once you have connected, focus on unconditional love. This is the energy of true guidance that many of us try to block. We have all kinds of ways of blocking it. Allow yourself to feel loved, allow yourself to accept this gift. If you do this for long enough, eventually your guide will be able to get through. Your guide is waiting for you to let down your armour and accept their help. They will never disarm you, and they will never interfere with your free will. This is why you will probably not be interested in receiving this kind of guidance until you are ready for it.

SAFEGUARDS WHEN WORKING WITH DISCARNATE GUIDES

Working with the energy of a personal guide is always safe. But if for any reason you feel unsure about whether or not you have established a true connection, you can ask the guide firmly who they are, and who is behind them. If you ask three times with intent, they will answer truthfully. The energy behind all true guides, including your personal spirit guides, is the energy of unconditional love. This energy is also called the Light of the Christ, the Great White Light or the Great Light. If this energy is not behind them, you have not connected with your guide. In this way you can ascertain if you have made a true connection, one that will benefit you.

The light of unconditional love is the same light that we find inside ourselves, the spark of light that we find through faith. This light dispels illusion, and its protection can always be relied upon. If you ever feel any need for protection, you can call upon it. The Christ Light is always there even if you can't see it or feel it. If you call upon it, it will protect you and bring you peace.

FINDING THE LIGHT OF GUIDANCE IN YOURSELF

You may choose not to be guided by a living guide, or by a teacher of the past, or by a guide from another level, but through your own inner light. The following exercise can help you connect to the guidance of your inner light.

Find a quiet space and time, sit comfortably with your feet on the floor and allow your body to relax. Breathe deeply and allow the breath to flow into your abdomen. Imagine little roots descending from your feet deep into the earth. Imagine a taproot attached to the bottom of your spine that goes down deep into the centre of the earth. Feel held by your roots, anchored to the earth. Bring up the healing energy of the earth as you breathe. Feel firmly held and grounded.

Focus on a point at the centre of your body, at your navel. Breathe deeply and feel a ball of warm light here at the centre of your being. Feel secure in your centre. Slowly, very slowly, bring this ball of light up to your heart centre. Breathe into this ball of golden light. Feel its warmth and radiance. Rest in your inner light.

Be aware that this light is your inner guide. It knows your deepest yearning and your most hidden fear. Your inner light is the essential part of you that is wise and loving. It knows that which you need to know in order to grow and evolve. It knows what you have gone through before, and it knows what you will go through in future. It is the light of your true wisdom, your true clear vision, a lantern within that can guide you home.

Focus on this light as you breathe, and then if you have a question concerning your path, your life purpose or your inner growth, show it to this light. If you are unsure of where you are going, ask this light to show you. If you are uncertain about others, ask this light to help you see them as they truly are. If you feel that you are stuck, ask this light to show you how to start to grow and evolve. Ask this light whatever you need to know. Ask with confidence that your request will be heard and an answer given.

Then open yourself to receive. Let the light in your heart spread out until it covers your chest. Breathe in the radiance of your inner light. Let yourself hear the truth that your own inner wisdom brings you. Receive the guidance you need. Do not strain to receive, relax and let it come to you. You may hear a voice, see a picture or symbol, or feel a sensation. Receive the impressions of your inner light and seek to understand the guidance hidden within them. Trust yourself.

You are a book that contains the universe. Open the first page of this book as you learn to receive guidance from within that reveals your true path. Have confidence in your own inner guidance. Everyone has access to their inner guidance but few people trust themselves enough to follow it. Trust your inner light to show you the way.

When you are ready to end this meditation, slowly become aware of your surroundings. Check that your feet are still firmly rooted to the ground. Open your eyes and make a commitment to remember and trust the guidance you have been given.

You can feed your inner light by an inner commitment to a more loving way of being. As you feel your inner light grow you will learn to trust it, and thereby become more attuned to inner guidance. You will learn to hear your heart's voice, and you will trust your heart's illumination to help you see clearly through illusion, to recognise your true purpose here. This purpose is in keeping with the nature of this light, which sees through everything to understand the true point, the point of grace, which is love and forgiveness.

With the step of guidance you choose to proceed either with the help of another's light, or with the assistance of your own. You are now ready to take your next step, the last step on the stair of faith. A new light illumines this step as you ascend, a light that falls from the window of sincerity.

THE WINDOW OF SINCERITY

Sincerity is the last step on the stair of faith, a step that leads to hope. The light of sincerity helps you be who you truly are. This light helps you to live without wearing a mask, to have just one face that you show to everyone, not a different face for every occasion. It helps you to say what you mean, and to do what you say, so that your being is a true reflection of what you say and do. The light of sincerity helps you to become integrated, to become one person, to become whole.

Without sincerity we have no centre, we change and shift as we weave our way through life, adapting to circumstances and people, but never really being true to ourselves. As we awaken to an awareness of our inner light our perspective on life changes. We are no longer blown about by everything that happens to us, as at the core of our being we sense a still centre of light. As we open to the inner warmth of our true self, we expand and radiate the love that lies hidden in our core. In this way we become who we really are, outer reflects inner, and we reveal our true face as we become sincere.

REASONS FOR STARTING A SPIRITUAL PATH

It is a good idea to look with sincerity at your reasons for starting a spiritual path. It may be that these will change as you progress. If you feel the need for a living guide, when you meet one they will look into the sincerity of your motives for seeking guidance, just as you will look into their motives for assisting you.

Some people are drawn to a path of return because they have a true calling. Through the ages individuals have responded to this call and followed a spiritual vocation within the confines of the cultural traditions of their time. There will always be those called to the spiritual path because they are born to do so. They will find their way, no matter what the circumstances of their lives, because this inner call is so strong that they can't ignore it.

Some less urgent motives for starting a path could be a desire to know yourself better, to become more aware, to become more fully human. You may want to further your growth, and to assist in the collective raising of consciousness at this time. You may want to get out of the trap of disharmonious relationships with others, to become more compassionate, to uncover the gentleness hidden in your heart. You may want to be more in control of your life, and to stop feeling at the mercy of your own and other people's misunderstanding.

A sincere desire for self-realisation may include both the desire to be free, and the desire to be of service. You may want to be free of the illusions that limit you, and to be of service to the rest of humanity. You may also start a path to find some peace; your need for a path may be a need for health and healing. You may realise that that your present way of life is making you ill, and that a spiritual path offers you a more harmonious way of living.

LESS POSITIVE MOTIVES FOR STARTING A PATH

A less positive motive might be the desire to progress on a spiritual path in order to become someone who will be able to attract and guide others. Another might be the desire to increase your charisma and personal power, by learning how to develop occult skills and perform miraculous feats. You may desire to know, to learn from the treasury of hidden esoteric knowledge. You may begin a spiritual path because you see it as a way of earning a living one day, or as a way of making new friends and contacts.

The desire to lead others is often motivated by inner feelings of worthlessness. This may drive individuals to prove to themselves that they are worthy of the love, respect, and even adulation of others. Although they may have advanced a certain distance, until they have healed their inner wounds, they are not ready to guide. They will use the love of seekers to assuage their own pain. In this way they will become tangled up, and not be connecting with the pure light of compassion, but with bonds of attachment and need.

The desire to acquire charismatic powers and perform miracles springs from the same root, which is a need to be loved and validated for what you can do, rather than loving yourself for what you are. Sometimes fear comes into it too, as people who fear domination may seek to master and control others, and their environment, in order to feel safe and in control of their world. Real liberation comes in the liberation from fear that enables us to be loving and vulnerable, knowing that love is the true power behind all being, behind all healing, and behind all grace.

The miraculous and healing nature of love is a miracle that is always shared. The nature of love is to share, to heal, to feed, and to sustain, from an inexhaustible supply. Once this is understood, miracles are seen as the natural order of love, and to live in accordance with love's law is to comply with love in every instant. This is the opposite to living in a state of limitation. To live in the awareness of love's power is to surrender to this power entirely, to give yourself to it. To be able to give yourself you must first heal from your own fear of being unloved and unlovable, and with the loss of this fear you also lose your limitations, your need to dominate your environment, and to control others.

To desire to know is a positive motive, but if knowledge is all that you want, you will not live what you learn. To really know spiritual truth is to live it with every breath. You cannot divorce what you know from who you are, and how you behave. If you try and keep them separate you will split yourself, and this split will prevent you from healing and becoming sincere. Knowledge without compassion loses its point; unless you discover a capacity to open up and trust, your path will lack warmth, and it will not bring you peace. However if you allow it to, the light of true knowledge can illumine your perception and open your heart. As you become truly wise your being will change, as you become more compassionate.

Those who start a path for future financial gain or to make new friends, may change their motives as time goes by. New friends can help you on your way, but if this is your only motive for starting out you will be concentrating all your energy outward, rather than inward. You will be looking around you, rather than cultivating the growth of your inner light.

FREEDOM FROM THE MATERIAL WORLD

True guides are free of the slavery of the material world because they have seen through it. They are not seduced by money, or enthralled by it, and they do not shun it or run away from it. They recognise that although the divine manifests through it, it is also a veil. They have seen through the veil of the material world to the truth behind it, which is unconditional love. They will guide you to this truth, and their guidance will reflect it. If you want to become a guide to make money, your guidance will be misleading. As a guide you will teach people how to become like you, not how to complete their evolutionary journey. However, it is possible that your motives will change, if you have a teacher who leads you towards compassionate truth. He or she will help you to see beyond purely material gain, to the greater gain of freedom and peace.

A PATH OF SELF-INTEREST

In choosing a path, and choosing a guide, you always have free will. If you want a path of self-interest, you will find a self-interested teacher who will teach you how to get what you want. You will learn to use other people to help you achieve your goals. You will not discover your heart's compassionate light, but this will not be what you want anyway. You will seek to dominate, to become master of yourself and others. This is your choice. There are many paths to grace, and there are many paths away from it. Be clear about what you want, define your motives. Then you will know where you are going, and you will not be misled like a child.

A PATH TO TRUTH

A guide to truth is one who has lost their self-interest in the interests of the whole. Such a guide, whether alive or in spirit, can help you to become more sincere, through their inner connection with you. Through their sincere direction you will be led towards less self-centred goals. Gradually the opening of your heart will enable you to experience your capacity for unconditional love, which will help you to become more human, to become more sane. A true guide has become sincere in intention and in being, and the light of their sincerity will help you to become like them.

If the spark of your sincerity increases you will find that your intentions change as you change, that your path is not what you expected, and that eventually you no longer want anything but love. You will also find that your path expands and affects all areas of your life, material, spiritual, and personal. You cannot have a spiritual path that encompasses only one part of you. All of you will be involved, as this is what happens when you become sincere. As you become sincere you will have less to hide. You will become the same person whoever you are with, and your consistency will be a sign of your spiritual progress.

FINDING THE LIGHT OF SINCERITY IN YOURSELF

If you want to become more sincere, you can start by becoming more honest. We lie all the time, to ourselves and to others. We lie with our thoughts, our words, our intentions and our actions. To begin to become more sincere is to start to realise how much we lie, and to lose the need to do so. Often we lie because we want something, and don't want to admit it openly, or because we're afraid that if we're honest we won't get it.

At root all of us want to be loved. On top of this there may be many layers of other things we want, because we fear our original need will not be fulfiled. The compensatory desires keep at bay our fear of unfulfilment - our fear of being unloved. As you understand that unconditional love is what you really want, let the other desires go. They are just a way of filling the void. Remember what you really want. This will help you become more sincere, more secure and more truthful.

Another way to begin to be more honest is to look at yourself candidly. Attempt to see through your pretence, to see the mixture of positive and negative traits within, and to accept your personality as it is. In this way you stop lying to yourself, for all of our personalities are a mixture of attractive and unattractive traits. Only when you have understood and accepted your own shadows can you understand the deeper beauty of your inner light.

Your heart holds this secret, as it tells you that beneath your transient identity you are a light, born to shine with love and sincerity, as is everyone else. The light in our hearts unites us, in the equality of love. Through beginning to see through your own lie, you begin to see by the light of your truth and this connects you to others. In this way you become sincere with others, and you begin to spread the sincerity of peace. One way you can tell when you are lying is by the way that you feel. If you are feeling peaceful, you are being sincere.

Some people follow a path of self-interest because they believe that no-one will ever love them for themselves. Everything that has happened to them in their lifetime confirms them in this belief. They may feel that there is no point in being human and compassionate, as others will abuse and exploit them if they are. But until you start to love someone else, you cannot escape from the grip of your own selfishness. It is a grip on your heart that stops you loving, and it stops you receiving anyone else's love. To loosen its grip you need to find the light beneath it, the light in your heart that reassures you that you are worthy of love, and that you can love others as your brothers and sisters. This light is faith.

THE NEXT STAIR ON THE TOWER OF GRACE

As the light of faith helps you become sincere, you are ready to move on to the next stage of your spiritual journey, the stage in which your ego is transformed. Without sincerity the ascent to the next stage is perilous. The stair of hope is a stage of upward movement. To follow a safe path, you need to be sincere before you start the climb. Your sincerity will give you stability, and ensure that others will benefit from your progress, rather than be trampled underfoot as you ascend.

Illumined by the light of sincerity you rise with confidence to the next stage of the tower. Behind you all the windows whose light you have received illumine the way. As you step onto the next stair, light streams down upon you from the window above, the window of hope.

THE STAIR OF
HOPE
2

The Window of Hope
◆
The Window of Aspiration
◆
The Window of Responsibility
◆
The Window of Trust

THE STAIR OF HOPE

**Where the ego is purified through
aspiration and transformed through trust**

The stair of hope is a stage of upward movement,
of rapid spiritual growth. At this stage you begin
to find conscious ways of connecting to your
source. Through sincere spiritual practice your
inner being is gradually illumined and purified. As
you progress, you begin to take responsibility for
your growth, and to understand its effect on others.
As you become mature enough to be spiritually
responsible, you become a helper, one who
assists others with a pure heart. Your outlook turns
from a self-interested orientation, to an orientation
that embraces the universe. Through this transformation you reach the step of trust, as you become
strong enough to hold a human trust, a trust of
peace that protects all life.

THE WINDOW OF HOPE

The next step on the tower of grace is hope. Without a sense of optimism it is difficult to sustain any endeavour, including a spiritual path. The voice of your despair is always ready to tell you that you're going nowhere, that you have made no progress. Through the step of hope you learn how to rise above this voice, and how to help others reach beyond despair. You take this step as you find a sense of purpose that brings you joy.

FINDING YOUR CALLING

To find a sense of purpose in your life is to find your true calling. Finding your calling means finding your soul's purpose, that which you are born to do. It is this that lifts you from the grip of broken dreams and sad regrets. It is never too late to find your calling. As you start to follow it, you find hope.

If you have no sense of purpose in your life you may live in a state of uncertainty that leaves you feeling scattered and in pieces. In this state every activity becomes a chore performed gracelessly, as you fight against time rather than flowing with it. To get back to a feeling of connectedness while being centred, of flowing with the universe and loving the energy of life around you, is to find your true calling.

Finding your calling really means finding the activity that best connects you to your divine source. Often people lose their way in life because through circumstances, or through the influence of others, they are diverted from their true course. Sometimes you may suffer physical or mental illness when the gap between your soul's true purpose, and what you are doing, becomes too great. The disconnection within you, this lack of contact with your source, leads you to live in a state of disease. Such times of illness provide an opportunity for an appraisal of your life so far, enabling you to find new ways of connecting. Connection brings health, as it brings your inner and outer being into alignment, an alignment that leads to a more harmonious integration of mind, body and spirit.

DIFFERENT WAYS OF CONNECTING TO YOUR SOURCE

Some people find a sense of connection through creativity, through the expression of their creative power, whether through the visual arts, the performing arts, literature or music. Being creative connects them to the creative energy of the universe. All of us are creative, and all of us have the capacity to tune into this universal energy in different ways. We may find a sense of connection through more homely creative activities such as gardening, sewing or cooking. What matters in any activity is the sense of connection, the feeling that you are in a stream of being, and that your outer activity mirrors your inner universe.

Some people find a sense of connection through healing, and they may be called to work in this field to deepen this connection. Healing is about connection, as the healer through channelling energy is able to connect to the energy of another person that may need recharging or rebalancing. Through this service the healer also becomes connected to the source of all healing, the universal energy that they channel.

Some may find their vocation in teaching, through the art of communicating and sharing ideas with other adults, or the next generation. A gifted teacher is able to connect with their pupils in such a way that the knowledge they impart affects their students like an electrical charge. It lights up their intelligence, increases their brightness, and makes them eager to learn more. Teaching is a joy when one connects to the intelligence of one's students, being able to inspire and illumine minds.

Some people find a strong sense of connection through their relationships with others. They may find a link to the divine through serving others, through looking after children, through caring for relatives or other people. Such individuals are nourished by their heart connection to those they care for, as in their work they find an avenue to their compassionate essence.

A passionate love relationship can also be an avenue to connection and grace. A marriage is truly blessed when the two individuals involved connect with each other and with the creative power of the universe through their union. A marriage is fulfiling when the divine is recognised in the mirror of the other person, and worshiped within an intimate relationship.

You may be called to pursue a spiritual path, a path that increases your inner light. You may wish to devote some of your time to contemplation and prayer. If your calling is spiritual, you will find that your path helps you uncover and radiate your inner light, so that others may benefit from the warmth of your spirit.

CONNECTION AS AN AVENUE TO HEALTH

Whether your calling involves silent inward activity, or is one that involves outward expression, or relatedness to others, it is the way it connects you to your centre that makes it valid. Your centre of peace is that within you which can feed and sustain you. It is the peace within you that never runs out. A true calling connects you to your inner light, to the divine spark within. It is this connection that makes the activity you have chosen an avenue to health, to peace, to blessing and to grace. It doesn't matter what the activity is. What matters is that it is the right one for you, it is the one that connects you to your centre. The thread of connection is always present in you, but until it is illumined you are not aware of it. A vocation is that which illumines your connection, lighting up your divine thread.

Nothing can sever this connection. You can choose not to feel it, you can choose to disconnect, you can choose a way of life that does not suit you. But the thread of your connection will not break; the avenue of your life's calling will never close. It will remain open, and this is why there is always hope. People love doing the activity that connects them best, as this is when they feel most alive. Your calling makes you feel good, as this is how you are essentially made to be, and connecting to your essence releases the goodness within you. If any activity brings you connection, it will also bring you joy, whereas if it doesn't it may bring you boredom, emptiness and fatigue.

A LIFE WITHOUT CONNECTION

Life without any connection to your divine source is ultimately dull; it is the connection of spirit to its source that brings you joy. If you work in the fields of teaching, healing or caring, and you have no connection to your inner light, it is easy to over extend your energy and become tired and drained. Such work requires that you find a means of connection to an energy source that supplements your own. Then your work will not exhaust you. If you have no access to your own inner pool of healing light, you may find that you have less and less to give.

A life without connection is a life without hope or joy, in which you feel tired all the time, and in which boredom is never far away. It can be so dull that many people find themselves seeking connection in activities that are ultimately self-destructive. Addictions or abusive relationships can provide a substitute for essential connection, a way of feeling temporarily alive, an excitement that is lacking from the rest of existence.

CONSTRUCTIVE AND DESTRUCTIVE CONNECTIONS

The first step for an individual in such a situation is to realise their need for a constructive connection, and to recognise that through making this connection they will be helped to get out of a self-destructive rhythm. A constructive connection links you to the positive energy of your inner light. A destructive connection links you to the negative energy of your inner shadow. Eventually on a spiritual path, light and dark combine in harmony, as you become more integrated. In the beginning however, it is important that you find a way to connect to your own light as this is your inner source of peace and healing. Other people in a self-help group can provide a point of positive connection, as the loving energy of the group can support you and strengthen your own light. Alternatively, you may find one activity, one pastime, talent or relationship that offers you a means of constructive connection, a lifeline to health.

FINDING A SOURCE OF CONNECTION IN YOURSELF

If your life seems to lack connection and hope, how can you find it? We all have our own calling although we may not hear it. To find your calling, the best means to connect and fulfil you, look at your life up till now. Then identify anything that brings you joy, any activity that you really love. If you can't think of anything then think ahead, imagine what you would like to be doing, in say, five years. Allow yourself to dream of what you would most enjoy doing with your life, this can be something very simple, or something elaborate. Be honest and find something that you really would enjoy, not something that would sound good to others.

If you can't think of anything that you want to do, think how you would like to feel. Focus on the way you would like to feel, and then think of what you could do with your time to foster this feeling. Do not be put off by practical considerations, by the responsibilities and demands of making a living in the world. If you feel a sense of connection through one thing in your life that you do for one hour a week, it will make a difference to the rest of the time. For that one hour you will have experienced the hope that connection brings. Once you have identified one thing, make a commitment to it.

You may decide to work voluntarily for a few hours a week in a profession such as teaching or healing. You may decide to create a work of art in a medium you have always wanted to explore. You may decide to grow a garden. You may decide to explore ways of connecting more honestly with your partner. You may decide to work with children, or bear a child. You may decide to do some kind of caring work, with other individuals, or with animals. You may decide to seek spiritual guidance, or you may ask to be guided through the power of universal love. You may decide to reorient your life, so that it has a deeper spiritual dimension. Whatever you decide to do, be prepared to make changes to your life, whether big or small, to accommodate your decision. Following your calling will bring you hope.

ACCESSING AN INNER SOURCE OF SPIRITUAL HEALTH

A sense of connection to your inner, and from your inner to your outer, makes your life harmonious and rich. If you are successful in your outer life but have no access to your inner well, you will feel empty. No amount of money, fame or success can make up for a lack of connection to an inner source of spiritual health. Without this connection you are always spiritually impoverished, no matter how much you have. It is the sense of connection to your source that is the real value you get from any activity, so it is worth looking at your motives for doing different things. That which is truly valuable is the growing sense of harmony and well being that comes from living in a state of connection.

The light of hope, from the window of this name, falls upon you as you reach this step on your spiritual journey. This light helps you find your life's true purpose, and your true direction. It helps

THE WINDOW OF HOPE

you follow this direction, and thereby evolve more gracefully and joyfully.

SHARING THE LIGHT OF HOPE WITH OTHERS

Having felt the light of hope, you can now give it to others. Other people can sense when someone is fulfilled in their life, and when they have a clear sense of purpose. You for your part probably know what it is like to feel disconnected, undecided, insecure and hopeless. By finding your calling you can help others find theirs, by encouraging them to listen to the calling of their soul, and to do what they really want to do with their lives. You can help them connect with their inner light, by sharing yours with them. You can share some of the positive energy you have found. To anyone who is falling into despair and hopelessness, you can lend a hand.

Climbing to the stair of hope, you discover that from now on your progress will no longer be yours alone. With every step you take on the second stair, you will take someone else with you. A spiritual path that is followed in isolation cannot take you very far. All true paths have this condition: when you have advanced a certain distance, your progress will be shared. In this way others will benefit from your increasing illumination, and your individual evolution will add to the evolution of the whole. If you are on a path of self-interest, the opposite will happen. If your path has no true destination, it will not involve you helping others, or giving them hope.

Feeling connected to your inner light and filled with hope, you are ready for the next step, the step of aspiration.

THE WINDOW OF ASPIRATION

The next window on the stair is aspiration. To aspire is to reach beyond where you are, to reach for your goal. Without aspiration you cannot proceed, for aspiration is the driving force behind movement and growth.

At first people may put great effort into their spiritual path to get somewhere, or become something. As they progress their perception usually changes and they realise that where they wanted to go, and what they wanted to be, are not their real goals any longer. As their heart opens they begin to experience their true spiritual identity, and are then able to hear the call of longing.

THE CALL OF LONGING

The call of longing is a call that kindles our aspiration. To hear the call of longing is to hear the cry of Love calling us back to Itself, a call that inspires us to return. It is a cry to which we respond, and our response is an echo of this primary call. Our longing is a reflection of the longing of unconditional love to be fully known. We as human beings are the medium, the instrument, through which the call of longing is received and returned.

As you reach the step of aspiration you may experience a longing for the Divine, for spirit, for your true self. You may experience this as a sense of longing for something outside of yourself. You may feel a sense of being pulled out of your everyday life towards your source, towards something true. You may recognise this feeling as a longing for God, for some contact with your inner truth, for the opening of your heart. If you do not know what you are longing for, you will feel restless and not know why. Your restlessness will be a symptom of your lack of satisfaction with all that the material world has to offer.

This feeling of longing for the divine is the root of many human relationships based on need. Once this is understood your dependence on other people may decrease, as you understand that your longing for them is just a projection of your longing for Truth. This doesn't mean that you will no longer care about anyone; it means that you will no longer burden your relationships with unreal expectations that others can never fulfil.

As you progress and begin to know your true self, you will recognise the true self in others and your relationships will begin to feel different. You will recognise the light hidden behind the forms of others, for you have recognised it in yourself. This understanding brings warmth as you connect with your centre, and with the centre of others. You no longer expect so much from people outwardly, and you no longer need them desperately.

THE NATURE OF YOUR ASPIRATION

The nature of your aspiration will dictate the level and speed of your progress on a spiritual path. If you aspire to become a spiritual person whom others will respect, your aspiration will limit you. If you aspire to become a trustworthy human being, your aspiration will ennoble you. If you aspire to experience divine unity, your aspiration will liberate you. If you aspire to nothing but love, your aspiration will help you leave all paths behind and return to your source.

The light of aspiration from the window of this name helps your aspiration become pure and true. It encourages your spirit to soar on wings of love, a flight that is glorious and free. You do not have to lead an outwardly spiritual life to aspire. You can live an ordinary life, and inwardly aspire beyond all bounds. The level of your aspiration is its own reward: for those with a lofty aspiration receive the assistance of all who reached for the heights before. They receive the spiritual breath of those who aspired beyond themselves, beyond the confines of their own time. This breath is one that carries you beyond yourself, beyond your everyday life in a fixed place and time. The light of this pure spiritual breath reaches you through this window on the stair.

FINDING THE LIGHT OF ASPIRATION IN YOURSELF

Before you can share the aspiration of timeless lovers, you have to prove yourself ready for this breath. Regular spiritual practice can help. Spiritual practice involves making a commitment to your inner light, a promise to remember it. By keeping your promise, by returning to your practice daily, you increase your inner illumination. Sincere spiritual effort is the effort of the heart and spirit to hear its voice, and reply to its own call of longing. It is progress towards integration, and is best achieved harmoniously. To progress upon a path you have to make some effort, but if this effort is motivated by longing, not by ambition, the progress made will be safer and purer.

If you have a sincere intention and would like to start some form of spiritual practice, then how can you begin? It is important to be consistent, and take a long-term view, because then you have a better starting point for a real change in your life. A true spiritual path involves gradual transformation. It takes a certain perseverance and patience to continue consistently in this way, taking time each day for your spiritual practice so that your life takes on a different rhythm, a different flavour.

Different people choose different forms of practice, and it's best to choose a method that suits you. The practice of meditation is a way of becoming more inwardly integrated and harmonious. There are several different forms of meditation, and many books, groups and teachers of different methods. If you find one of these suits you, go ahead and practice it consistently for about half an hour a day.

MEDITATION ON THE BREATH OF LIGHT AND THE HEART OF LIGHT

Here is a simple method of meditation that you can try if none of the others suit you. To practice it find a quiet place and set aside some time when you will not be disturbed. Sit in a chair with your feet on the floor, and your spine straight. Feel roots descending from the soles of your feet, deep into the earth. Feel the energy of the earth grounding you, holding you steady. Then focus on your breath. Breathe deeply and let your breath help you find your centre. Breathe deeply from your centre, and let your body relax as you breathe.

As you breathe in take in the positive energy around you, imagine you are breathing in a stream of golden light, the energy of love. Feel this energy filling your centre, warming you and healing you. As you breathe out release this golden energy, in the knowledge that there will always be plenty more of it to take in, for it never runs out. When you feel warm and peaceful move on to the next part of the meditation.

As you breathe in imagine your breath going straight to your heart and filling it with golden light, with the energy of unconditional love. As you breathe out let your breath proceed from your golden heart out into the atmosphere around you. Feel your positive energy blessing your surroundings with golden light. The energy of blessing is the energy of unconditional love. We all have a means of access to our inner light, through the blessing of our breath.

Continue to breathe in this way, in consciousness of your heart of light. Gradually come back to everyday awareness. The light of the heart is positive energy, and it is this energy that you will focus on and increase through this form of meditation. Without an inner store we soon become depleted; people tire us and we lose patience. If you increase your inner store of light daily, you will have a reserve that will help you to cope with the demands of your outer life, demands that test your good will. You will have more energy to care both for yourself and others.

If you do this exercise regularly you will find that eventually your heart warms up, and you will feel the heat in your chest as you draw in and send out universal love. After some years, you may find yourself doing the breath and heart of light through your day, not just in meditation. You will become a source of blessing, as this is the nature of the energy of love that is transforming and healing you. Eventually your heart will always be alight, and you will share your light with others.

ASSESSING THE BENEFIT OF YOUR SPIRITUAL PRACTICE

A good way to ascertain whether the practice you are doing is bringing you any real benefit is to consider how you have changed since you started it. If you have become more calm and centred, and more patient and understanding with others, then your practice is helping to illumine your inner being and purify your heart. If you have become more self-obsessed and driven, and more irritated with others, your practice is not helping you increase and share your inner light.

Your practice will hinder your spiritual progress if it makes you feel purer, higher and more spiritually evolved than others who don't have a regular practice, or a spiritual path. Pride and arrogance are walls that rise up to shield you from the gentleness of your heart's light. Your practice will begin to have an element of strain, and you will attach excessive importance to it, and to any states you experience while practising. You may have many of these, but they will be gifts that you cannot share. As you continue to practice, this wall of pride will become denser and thicker so that you receive less and less illumination from within.

RECOVERING FROM SPIRITUAL PRIDE

The way to bring down an inner wall of pride is to realise your insignificance before creation. As long as you think you are the centre you will be unable to feel part of the flow of life. Part of feeling this flow is to feel the flow of your breath in true spiritual practice. This practice unites you to all life, in a loving breath of compassionate grace. To remember love with every breath is to feel held within the embrace of all life, for all life comes from the energy of love. So if you are proud of your practice, you have not yet learned to breathe with humility and become part of life's flow. When you learn to do this, your practice will come into tune with the rest of life, and it will lead you to become more inwardly harmonious. A sign of this is that you will become calmer, more patient and humble, and your relationships with others will become less fraught.

Meditation is just one form of spiritual practice; some people respond more actively to the call of longing. They may sing, or dance, as a way of celebrating their love for the divine. If a person's song is a way of relating to their divine essence, it doesn't matter if it is not heard or appreciated by others. What matters is the sincerity of the one who sings, plays music, dances or recites poetry.

SINCERITY OF INTENTION IN SPIRITUAL PRACTICE

Without sincerity of intention, all forms of practice are empty of spiritual value, no matter how perfectly they are performed. Sincere spiritual practice is never about performance, it is about feeling. The one whose love is strongest will benefit most from any form of spiritual practice; for their practice is motivated by a true longing, and their sincerity gives it lasting value.

Such practice is the income that you earn on a spiritual path. Sincere practice increases your store of inner illumination, and helps you make peace with yourself and others. If your practice is not sincere, if you are meditating or singing to reach a higher level, or in order to be seen to do so, you may achieve this level, but your progress as a whole will lack depth. This is because spiritual practice that is motivated by ambition cannot lead to real transformation. It may lead you to become adept, but it will not lead you to an understanding of the true purpose behind all practice. Only deep transformation, the transformation of being, can lead you to ultimate meaning, to the understanding of yourself and the point of your path.

However, it is possible to change the nature of your practice if your intention becomes sincere, or if someone else guides you whose practice is sincere. You may then open up to the attractive force of longing. Once open to this, your practice will be motivated by love, not by vanity or ambition.

If you are on a true path, you will progress to greater depth of being as you understand the purpose behind all practice, and the responsibility inherent in becoming more adept. This responsibility is towards all creation, but also towards those whom you are close to in everyday life. If your spiritual practice cuts them out, leaves them behind, or makes you feel superior to them, it will not change you in a positive way. If your spiritual practice teaches you how to become more tolerant towards those around you, if it helps you to help them, you are ready for your next step. This is the step of responsibility.

THE WINDOW OF RESPONSIBILITY

The step of responsibility anchors your aspiration in service. You become responsible, as you realise that your spiritual path has an effect on others, and that your increasing spiritual strength can benefit the whole. Unless you learn to help others on their journey in some way, it is easy to lose the point of your own.

Through treading a spiritual path, you will have begun to look at events in your life differently. Through forgiveness you will have started to heal your history; through sincerity you will have become more integrated. Through hope you will have seen beyond a tendency to despair, and you will have learned how to connect with an inner source of spiritual nourishment. Through aspiration you will have learned to celebrate your inner light, and to see beyond your own ambition. Your path so far has been a path of healing, of healing wounds and splits and discordant notes in your inner tune. To begin to heal is to move closer to equilibrium, to begin to find a sense of inner balance. If you reach the step of responsibility you will have healed yourself sufficiently to be able to help others. This does not mean that your healing will be complete, or that you can help others to heal completely. However you will have reached a stage on your journey where you can assist another, and assisting them will further your own growth.

BECOMING SPIRITUALLY MATURE

Becoming responsible involves choosing to help carry the burdens that others are not strong enough to carry alone. Whether you chose to be a helper or not depends on whether you have matured enough to understand the responsibility inherent in spiritual growth. If you have not, you will shun this step, and you will not rise beyond a lonely aspiration. If you have, then you will learn how to be a helper to your own kind. Until you take this step you cannot reach the stage of trust.

When you help another, this service will help you to grow in compassionate understanding. It will not halt your progress or drag you down. If you shun the responsibility involved in becoming a helper, you will not yet have understood the ultimate purpose behind all growth, which is universal grace and healing.

If you are on a true path, you will stay stranded on the step of aspiration until you become mature enough to take responsibility for your own growth. If however, your path has no true point, at this stage you may well take a wrong turn. As you develop your spiritual and psychic abilities, you develop a greater sense of autonomy, and a more precise and lucid perception of the reality behind everyday life, and everyday relationships. This increased perception, and increased sense of mastery, will give you a certain strength. If your path has an occult element, it may be now that you learn how to use your abilities for both good and ill. Energy is not bad or good, its use is what makes it positive or negative. A positive use of energy is useful to the whole; it heals by bringing together, and unity is its aim. A negative use of energy is detrimental to the whole, pulling apart rather than bringing together, and is ultimately destructive.

A PATH WITHOUT RESPONSIBILITY

Some paths will lead you nowhere; they will just waste your time. Some paths will lead you to become human, to share the compassionate light in your heart. And some paths will rob you of light and faith. I mention this for the sake of those who are unsure, so that they may ask questions and decide for themselves if their path is taking them somewhere that they want to go.

Teachers whose motives are self-interested have no energy of grace and blessing to sustain their spiritual life. They will sustain their spiritual energy through consuming the light and innocence of their new students. This is the parasitic reality behind paths of self-interest. Most people on such a path do not see this reality until much later on, when they become teachers themselves.

If you are on a self-interested path and you decide to leave, this is the time to do so, while you still can. For the next step on your path will make leaving more difficult. Your next step will be the opposite of responsibility; it will involve the irresponsible use of power. You will learn how to flatter, seduce, corrupt, intimidate and harm other people. You will have increasing contempt for those less adept than you, whom you will learn to manipulate with ease, through your mastery of the etheric level.

You may believe that your aim is personal freedom, but until you can trust yourself you are never free. Without responsibility for your own actions and their effect on the whole, you cannot reach the step of trust. You will be unwilling to bear anyone else's burdens, and you will learn to manipulate and use other people so that they carry yours. You will learn to exploit others, just as you were exploited. You will become like your teachers, for this is all they can teach you, how to become like themselves.

ASSESSING THE TRUE NATURE OF YOUR PATH

At this stage your own spiritual health will tell you what kind of path you are on, and where it is going. If you are on a path that leads you nowhere, you will not have changed. You will be as you were when you began.

If you are on a self-interested path you will have become more ill at ease, restless, vain and overbearing. You will expect others to respect you. The knowledge that you can use (and abuse) power will feed your growing sense of mastery. You will feel strong, but although confident of your strength, you will fear those whose occult power is greater than yours. No-one will be allowed to penetrate your barriers, not even those with whom you are most intimate. Your heart will harden, and you will lose what little gentleness you had before.

If you are on a human path, at this stage you will experience a feeling of good will, of generosity of spirit. You will have healed enough to want to help your own kind; you will not feel above them, just fortunate to have found some light to share. You will tread a path of patience and humility, and your sense of contentment will increase. You will feel open to love and gentleness and you will be able to be vulnerable with others. You will fear no one, no matter how great their occult power. You will trust in the Christ light, the light of faith and peace within you, for this is your protection from illusion, and from harm. You will tap into a deep well of inner peace, as you taste the beauty of true service on a path to grace.

The light of responsibility that falls from the window of this name, is one that takes you beyond a self-interested aspiration. It will show you the way to be of service to your own kind. This light is one that leads you to give others right guidance, to put their interests before your own.

FINDING THE LIGHT OF RESPONSIBILITY IN YOURSELF

If you would like to become more responsible in a spiritual sense, what can you do? For a short space of time each day, endeavour to lose yourself in someone else's life. We have been taught to lose ourselves in our ambition, in our work, in our sense of purpose, in our goals. We have not been taught to lose ourselves in compassion, in understanding, in brotherhood. Such a loss is always a true spiritual gain.

You will find that, with practice, to take a real interest in another person is not such an effort. For example, you may be given the chance to help someone, but feel too tired to become involved. You may be asked for advice, and be tempted to reply in clichès because it's easier, rather than deeply feeling the pain of another person. You may be asked to lend a hand in a practical sense, but this may inconvenience you. You may be called upon to support someone through a period of despair, through a deep grief. You may be given the opportunity to trust someone, or to let them trust you. You may be called upon to give another person some light, to share a little hope.

All of the above involve a choice, and it is how you handle this choice that will demonstrate your capacity to be responsible in a spiritual sense. If you respond with your heart, and forget your own goals for a moment while caring for another, your path will have brought you to this step.

To really care for another person enough to carry their load for a while has always been an avenue to grace. Such caring purifies your aspiration and changes your path. For by caring enough to forget yourself, you give someone else a little faith, a little hope. You open the door for them to find their way. It does not require that you do anything heroic or even outwardly noticeable, it is really an attitude of heart. This attitude is one of compassionate responsibility that leads you to become a servant of humanity. To become a servant of humanity means that you become a helpful step on the ladder of evolution, and it ensures that your spiritual growth will benefit others. This attitude teaches you how to be generous, how to share. If you never learn this attitude you either stand still on your path, or you turn away from grace.

THE STEP OF RESPONSIBILITY

The step of responsibility is wet with the tears of those who understood for the first time the beauty inherent in a path of service. It is easy to slip on the step below, if your aspiration makes you proud. You can lose your footing through arrogance, and fall. The path becomes both more beautiful, and more perilous, the higher you climb.

From the step of responsibility you look ahead to the stairs above. The next step is a wide one, and beside the window there is an arch framed by unlit candles. Carefully you climb from the step of responsibility to the step of trust. You take with you the blessing of all of those whom you have helped, all those to whom you have given a little faith and a little hope. Through becoming responsible for the welfare of others, you reach the step of trust.

THE WINDOW OF TRUST

The light from this window illumines your sense of purpose, your spiritual aspiration, and your human nature. As you grow in connectedness to all life your path becomes part of everyone's path, and theirs becomes part of yours. You lose much of your self-interest because it no longer serves any useful purpose, and in this way your ego is permanently transformed. If you begin to take responsibility for your growth, and to share the benefit of this growth with others, you will start to connect more deeply with all life. Until you feel a sense of friendship and loving connection to all life, you cannot feel at peace with the world and its inhabitants. With the step of trust you wake up to the blessing of being alive.

THE TRUST OF BEING HUMAN

From the step of responsibility you arrive at the step of trust. Becoming worthy of trust means becoming fully human. To become fully human is to become someone who can no longer hurt or harm other forms of life. Any pain that you inflict you feel as your own pain, through your sense of connection to the whole. A fully human being is not able to cause pain to others, because they feel this pain themselves. The trust that you accept as you take this step is one that safeguards and reveres all life. Becoming trustworthy is about becoming a brother or sister to all created being, and keeping the trust inherent in this relationship.

The material realm is a realm where fear and conflict intermingle with love and harmony, where spirit intermingles with matter, and light with dark. All of these opposites are expressions of the same energy, the energy of love in its own process of self-consciousness. As we become more conscious we begin to unite these opposites within ourselves, and begin to express the grace that is their origin. Our sound understanding now springs from an understanding of the evolutionary process that we have undergone so far. This is the understanding that makes us unable to hurt or exploit our brothers and sisters, the animal life around us, or our environment. It is an understanding that brings us a trust of peace. In a real sense we stand under creation and hold it up.

This is the trust that in mythological terms was given to our first parents, to Adam and Eve, and which they forgot how to hold. We remember this trust as we remember that every human being has a sacred trust to uphold and share. To hold the trust of humanity is to understand our unique place in creation as the guardians and protectors of life on earth. This trust is not a trust of force, it is a trust of peace. As each of us begins a personal journey of self-recovery, we aid the recovery of our planet, and of humanity. As we accept a sacred trust to heal and protect, and not to harm and exploit, we remember the trust that Adam forgot. In this way we help to heal the fall from grace of the whole human family.

PATHS WITHOUT THE STEP OF TRUST

Any path that does not lead to trust, to the trust of being human and unable to cause harm, will lead you round in circles. Although you may think you have learned much, none of your learning will ultimately benefit you. You will waste your time in circular patterns of egocentric behaviour. The way out of such a circle is to transcend your own self-interest. Until you do, you will remain in a circle of fear, where the most dominant creature holds sway. Your spiritual path will reflect this predatory dynamic, as will the rest of your life. The way out of an aggressive, fearful and ultimately pointless circle, is to step outside it with trust. This step renders you vulnerable, and yet it does not make you weak. It makes you human.

If you are on a self-interested path, this is the stage at which you will become a broken step on the evolutionary ladder. No one will be able to trust you. You will no longer be able to trust yourself, for you will be unsure of your own limits. Having lost your conscience on the previous step, you will have no self-restraint. Nothing will prevent you from a path of vicious self-interest. You will dance to the tune of your own shifting desires, a dance motivated by restlessness and fear.

As you can no longer trust yourself, you will trust nobody else. You will expect their motives to mirror yours. The world you live in will be a world without faith and trust, and your dance will be fuelled by desperation. You will teach others to dance this way also. You will hook them by their attraction to money, sex or power, and these will be the idols that you dance around. They will discover some time in the future, that you were not worthy of their trust, and that your dance robbed them of peace.

THE DANCE OF GRACE

The dance of grace is the dance of a free spirit. It is the dance of creation of which you are a part. To hear the tune of grace you must first learn to live in harmony with the rest of creation, and choose not to damage it. You have to learn to love others with a love that respects their divinity, and that does not reduce them to objects. The melody of grace lies in the heart, it is the song of our innocence that loves creation and cannot lay it to waste. This is the song of a trust that we ceased to hold, but that we can learn to hold again, if we so choose.

FINDING THE LIGHT OF TRUST IN YOURSELF

If you would like to expand your path, so that you become more fully human and trustworthy, it can help to remember some of the times when you were not. We all have within us the capacity to be cruel, and to think only of ourselves. As the light of faith increases in your heart, and a feeling of sincerity increases in your spiritual practice, you may start to look around you with a new sense of responsibility. Trust is about being responsible for your words and actions, so that you come to know yourself well enough to be able to trust yourself.

To be able to trust yourself is to know that a connection to all life sustains you and keeps you sane, and that once you lose this connection, you can no longer be trusted. Looking over the past, understanding and forgiving yourself for your lack of connection, is one way to heal the lack of balance that has been your true state until now. The next step is to feel a sense of brotherhood with all living beings, because your sense of connection renders you open to loving them, as much as you love your self. In other words you start to love all life, and to hold it in the same regard as you hold your own life.

This is a big step on any one's path, for it means that you have turned from loving yourself towards a greater love, the love of all life. Without the step of trust a spiritual path lacks nobility. True nobility is that which elevates the human soul to a level beyond cruelty, greed and self-interest. As long as we are only living for ourselves, we have no integrity, and we cannot be trusted.

BECOMING WORTHY OF TRUST

As you receive the light of trust from the window of this name you become someone whom others can rely on; you become straight-forward and honest. You no longer see yourself as the centre of the universe, but understand your place in the wider scheme. You become a caretaker of the earth, and are able to take up Adam's trust, as you become willing to love and protect all life. You are illumined by the same light that illumines others who have recognised their humanity, and who have learned to love as you have. You become part of a human brother and sisterhood, the noble fraternity of those who love beyond themselves and their own interests. This means that you are unable to inflict pain on other forms of life, or to exploit any living being for reasons of personal gain.

Becoming trustworthy means that you will not be able to disrespect the humanity of others. You will not be able to take advantage of other people financially, emotionally or sexually. You will not be able to threaten or intimidate anyone. You will become someone who can be trusted as a friend, someone whose motives are pure. Becoming a person worthy of trust means that you lose your self-importance. In truth however, you have taken one of the most important steps of your life. Now you will find yourself on a human path, the path of those who hold the balance for the rest of their kind. You hold the balance, for your spiritual attitude is in direct opposition to an attitude of self-interest that motivates most people.

THE COUNSEL OF PEACE

Through becoming trustworthy you become a peacemaker, one whose word is true, and whose motives are pure. You spread the light of trust whoever you are with, and you bring to others the counsel of true brotherhood. This is the counsel of peace, the counsel that can always be trusted. Thus you become a true healer, one whose role in creation is to heal and mend, to bring together, to bring peace. It doesn't matter if you don't work in the healing arts. Your presence will now bring a healing influence wherever you go, and whatever you do.

Those who have reached the stage of trust are those who have transcended a self-motivated path, and become the torchbearers of their kind. This company has no outward organisation, and you may not even know that you belong to it. If your being has evolved enough that you feel the pain of others as your own, and you are unable to exploit or cause harm to any living being, then you have proved yourself worthy of the trust of peace. You are now given a burning torch, the torch of trust, from one who stands beside you on the stair. You realise as you take the torch, that the step of trust is one you found because others held a torch for you.

THE TORCH OF TRUST

If there were no trustworthy human beings left on earth, humanity would be left without the torch of trust. Without trust no human society can hold together for long, and neither can a human family. Without trust in yourself, you have no integrity either. Without trust we break up, for nothing is sacred when trust is broken. For this reason there have always been torchbearers, human beings who held a sacred trust for the rest of us. They helped to hold the spiritual balance between light and dark on earth.

You now carry the burning torch of trust, for the sake of all of those on the stair below. Your spiritual purpose now encompasses the healing of the planet and its people, as by becoming a torchbearer you now play your own small part in this endeavour. By the end of the stair of hope your ego has been transformed, and your path has ceased to be purely personal and now contributes to the evolution of the whole.

The next stage of your path is the stair of kindness. On this stair you will grow to know and understand the flaws hidden in your heart, that threaten your trustworthiness. You will learn to heal these flaws so that you become spiritually strong, a human being who can permanently hold a sacred trust. Without self-knowledge you cannot hold the trust of peace for long, for you will not be strong enough, or wise enough, to hold it.

Holding the flaming torch of trust you light the seven unlit candles around the arch ahead of you. These candles signify the steps traversed so far: faith, forgiveness, guidance, sincerity, hope, aspiration and responsibility. As the seven candles illumine the archway, more light falls on the dark stairs below. In this way others on the stairs of faith and hope are given light, through the progress of one who goes ahead of them. You now walk through the arch of trust, bearing a flaming torch. As you reach this portion of the staircase the tower becomes less gloomy and dim. Through the window of kindness you see the sun rising. A rosy dawn now warms the interior of the tower.

THE STAIR OF KINDNESS

Climbing onto the stair of kindness, you walk into a lighter, warmer world. Kindness transforms your path. Around this window crimson roses climb, and you hear the song of a bird outside. The stair of kindness is reached with relief, as the long night is over. This does not mean, however, that you can no longer fall. You climb to this stair with faith and hope, but you are aware that these can still be lost. On the rose scented stair of kindness your heart will be tested and made pure, so that you are able to hold a lasting trust.

THE STAIR OF
KINDNESS

The Window of Kindness
❖
The Window of Tranquillity
❖
The Window of Courage
❖
The Window of Patience

THE STAIR OF KINDNESS

**Where the heart is purified through kindness
and transformed through patience**

At the stage of trust your direction changes, as you are no longer on an ego-oriented path. At this point your path ceases to be purely upward, and starts to expand. From the centre of your being you expand, as you experience your connection to all life. This movement reflects a change in your outlook and your goals. You are no longer concerned with getting to the top; you are more interested in embracing all life and understanding it.

This change in direction is a sign that your ego has been permanently transformed, and that you are ready for the next stage of the journey. This is a stage where you learn to be spiritually strong. Spiritual strength is strength of being, the strength of those who have mastered themselves. It is learned in the school of the heart, where you come to recognise and heal the splits in your character that make you spiritually weak. Such a process of healing can only work if it is motivated by kindness, for you cannot heal your nature through attacking yourself. Through understanding and self-knowledge you become humble, wise and strong.

By the end of this stair your heart will be illumined and pure. A pure heart holds the trust of humanity in its light. To hold the torch of trust for a lifetime, you need to possess humility, courage, patience and integrity. This is the trust that Adam lost, as he forgot the light hidden in his heart, a light that radiates compassion. As you heal your character you come to realise the worth of this light, the light of those who share a lasting trust.

THE WINDOW OF KINDNESS

Rising to the stair of kindness you pass into a warmer world. On this stair your spiritual weaknesses are revealed, and through self-knowledge you learn how to heal them. As you heal them, you become spiritually strong. Spiritual strength reveals itself in humility, kindness, tranquillity, patience, integrity, courage and sincerity. These qualities are strengthened as you recognise their opposites within yourself, and bring them into balance. Such a process does not involve zealous self-criticism, but gentle self-understanding.

In the following chapters I will look at the different kinds of sickness that can afflict your spirit. I will look at the antidotes, the avenues to healing, the means whereby you can return to spiritual health. Without spiritual health we have no light, for our hearts are not sound and pure. Only a sound heart can radiate the light of a human trust.

THE SPIRITUAL SICKNESS OF PRIDE

The most common sickness found in the heart is pride. The seed of pride takes root as soon as you begin to see yourself as better than others, in some way special. As you mature, you either learn to manage this weed and train it, or you let it overrun your inner garden. I will give an example of how pride can weaken your heart and spirit, and inhibit inner growth.

Imagine that you become very successful in a chosen career. You may have a special talent, through which you excel. Other people are impressed, and you gain status and recognition. This all sounds positive, but it is the effect that this process can have on your inner being that may cause trouble. Being successful and respected is good if your heart remains sound. However, it is an unusual person who can see through their own success, and the admiration of others, to understand the danger hidden within it. People become inwardly weakened not by success, nor by the reactions of others, but by a hidden seam within their own hearts. This seam holds the seeds of pride, that all of us possess. When others start to admire and flatter you, this seam splits open and the seeds of pride pop out. If you are wise you will be aware of the danger, and train the growing seeds as they take root. If you are less spiritually experienced you may not be aware of the seeds of pride growing within, until they have become a thicket of strong and wayward vines.

SYMPTOMS AND EFFECTS OF THIS SICKNESS

As you become more proud, your motives will become less pure. You will begin to be curious about what people say about you, and you may start doing things in order to be noticed and admired. You may start to expend a lot of energy projecting the image of yourself that you want others to see. As you do so you will lose the ability to look within and reflect on your own behaviour. You will become less able to accept criticism, and you will always seek to justify yourself. You may become short tempered and brittle with people close to you, as you become full of self-importance. If anyone challenges you it may be those close to you in private who bear your irritation, as in public you will wear a different face. Your hubris will begin to infect your inner being, and you will lose all sincerity as the vine takes hold.

Pride unchecked leads to blindness and coldness, for the very proud cannot see beyond themselves, and their arrogance extinguishes their heart's warmth. Your achievements from now on will have a barren brilliance, for without vision and warmth, you cannot inspire others to succeed. The vine of pride strangles any hope of honest intimacy with other people, for the very proud cannot deeply connect with anyone. Their outer success hides their inner poverty, for pride strips them of self-awareness, vision, warmth and meaningful human contact.

THE DANGERS OF SUCCESS

It is dangerous to court success in any field, until you have fully recognised the tendency to pride and arrogance that is hidden in the human heart. Until you recognise this tendency, you may not be able to train the vine once it starts, or release yourself from its grip once it has taken hold. If this happens to you, it is best to leave behind the path to success for a while, and find instead a path to healing.

YOUR SOUL'S TRUE PURPOSE

True success is found not in what you do, but in the recognition of who you are. Everyone has a unique contribution to make to creation, and to make your own contribution is the reason you were born. However pride and greed often get in the way, and you may lose sight of your original goal. Your soul's true purpose is never at odds with the purpose of the whole. Your true purpose is always in harmony with the evolutionary growth of everyone else. The part of you that is proud is the part of you that wants to split off from the whole. To reconnect with creation is to understand your essential worth, and your personal insignificance.

RECOGNISING YOUR TRUE WORTH

True humility is not about feeling less than you are, or less than anyone else. It is about recognising your true worth. You are worth the light that makes you human. Everything else you have you can lose, but you cannot lose this. You become humble as you learn to kneel before the altar of your true light, and see through the borrowed brilliance of all else. As you feel the grace of your heart's compassion, light from the window of kindness illumines the way before you.

Understanding your insignificance in the cosmos will keep you well, as this understanding unites you to the whole again. The swelled head of pride belongs to one who thinks they are the centre of creation; this makes them blind, cold and ultimately foolish. Recognising your essential worth, you are able to reconnect to all life with kindness, as you share your light. You can then recover from the delusion of being separate that caused you to fall from being human.

THE NOURISHMENT OF THE HEART

To lose the need to feel better than others is to find your need for love. Alone before creation you stand proud. But the heart longs for companionship, understanding and brotherhood. To understand your human need for love is to let down your defenses and begin to nourish your heart. Without kindness towards yourself and others, you cannot heal. You cannot heal through being anything but gentle to yourself, to others, and to your children.

Any path without kindness will lead you to pride. Pride will always lead you into a bitter cold blindness. The damage that you do in your blindness damages you by destroying your own integrity, so that you cannot carry a light for anyone, you cannot keep anyone's trust. Spiritual health is found in a heart that has trained the vine of pride, and turned pride's bitter berries into the sweet wine of kindness.

THE HEALING POWER OF KINDNESS

Sometimes a time of crisis can lead you to discover the healing power of kindness. Through the influence of a proud heart you may begin to split from the whole, not in reality (this is impossible) but in your human consciousness. When the delusive split becomes too great some people have nervous breakdowns, physical illnesses, or periods of deep depression. These mental or physical sicknesses may be opportunities for you to recognise your purpose here, and to heal your body, heart and mind.

At times of crisis, if you are lucky, you may receive kindness from another human being, which helps you to heal. You may then find that you can no longer hold back from loving those around you whom you have treated for too long without kindness. That is why such times can become a breakthrough to true healing, as long as you are not treated by those who have not yet healed themselves.

Kindness affects you when you are vulnerable, and it makes you gentle. This gentleness enables you to be gentle to others whom you have previously wronged. It enables you to ask for forgiveness, and to forgive yourself, for past cruelty. Cruelty goes hand in hand with pride; it is the fruit of a bitter vine. Gradually as you make amends, gentleness washes over your being and heals the scars of a cruel heart. Through the power of gentleness, your inner split begins to mend and heal. Instead of being divided your heart becomes whole, and begins to radiate a human light.

FINDING THE LIGHT OF KINDNESS IN YOURSELF

Attempt to make every day a day when you connect with someone with kindness. This is not so different from the exercise for the first step of the path, that of faith, but the difference now is the level of your understanding. You understand how lost and ill you are without kindness. You understand how all spiritual practice is shallow without kindness. You understand how kindness makes you responsible, and how hollow is guidance if not motivated by kindness. You understand how forgiveness cannot be real, faith cannot be found, nor trust kept, without it.

In this way you understand the steps you have taken, and the windows you have passed beneath, through the perspective of your own heart's growth. In this way you come to understand that kindness underpins any genuine spiritual path, that it is part of every step, and that a path without kindness will lead you to the wilderness. This is where you find yourself if you lose your way through pride. Most of us do at some time; for this reason you are always helped by those who lost their way before. They understand, and treat you with kindness, as this is how they were helped to recover.

THE MEDICINE FOR A PROUD SPIRIT

The light of kindness from the window of this name brings you back from an inner wilderness to a path to grace. The way to ensure that you don't end up there again is to remember every day the power of this gentle light. Feel a connection to others through your heart's kindness. This is the medicine that heals a proud spirit. Your growth in kindness is the true measure of your spiritual health. The kinder you are, the more light you have to share, and the less you have to fear.

THE STEP OF TRANQUILLITY

The next step on the tower of grace is the step of tranquillity. As you approach this step the wind outside the tower begins to howl, the sky goes dark, and a storm begins. The torch of trust that you carry begins to flicker, as gusts of wind rush through the window arches of the tower. You can only reach the step of tranquillity when you have weathered your inner storm. This is the storm that will assail you as you approach the next step, and that with help, you will learn how to calm.

THE WINDOW OF TRANQUILLITY

The light of tranquillity illumines a pure heart that has waged its own battles, and found its own strength. You cannot grow spiritually without experience of life, hiding from situations that challenge your calm. Life involves a series of initiations that mark your increasing spiritual maturity. These initiations are not usually formal, but are the result of experiences in which the soul is tempered and the heart purified. Through difficult situations we grow in wisdom and love. Sometimes, this learning process involves an element of personal suffering. However this suffering is a means to an end, the end being increased understanding, and an increased capacity to love.

STEPPING STONES ON A COMPASSIONATE PATH

An increase in compassion is the real purpose behind all spiritual growth, and the initiations we undergo are the stepping stones that lead us to this goal. A heart that is perfectly loving is perfectly illumined, tranquil and pure. It has an endless stream of light to share. To reach this stage of illumination, you may have to go through many lifetimes of learning, and sometimes of struggle. The further you progress the more you have to go through, and the stronger you become.

It follows then, that on your path you will be confronted with situations that test you, and that force you to experience in practice that which you have learned about in theory. A spiritual path must be experienced, not merely talked about, read about, or written about. This means that you may encounter turbulence and upheaval in your personal life. You will meet individuals who will teach you, in one way or another, the lessons you need to learn. They will reveal to you the sides of your nature that have not yet been transformed. In meeting whatever challenges they bring, you will discover the worth of all that you have already learned.

There are many ways in which your inner peace can be challenged, just as there are many qualities within you that can cloud the purity of your heart. One quality that will threaten your inner peace is the storm of your selfish desire. You cannot be completely trustworthy until you have felt the power of this storm, and learned how to calm it.

THE SPIRITUAL SICKNESS OF SELFISH DESIRE

Selfish desire is about consumption. It is a restless craving that is never satisfied. Whether this desire manifests in addiction, using people, or a longing for material possessions, the driving force behind it is a restless desire to consume. It is this lust to consume that is transformed by the light of tranquillity, into a state of contentment and peace.

I will now give an example of how lust can raise a storm within you, and how you can see through this storm, as you learn to calm it. I will use the scenario of a student/teacher relationship for this example; however this particular theme is played out in many different contexts in daily life.

THE ENLIGHTENED LAW OF LOVE

If you are a young aspirant on a spiritual path you may be unaware that your spiritual teachers may not yet have learned to master their own selfish desire. You may come under the influence of a teacher who is not trustworthy. To be completely trustworthy is to have transcended a selfish way of being. If the inner being of your teacher is pure and trustworthy, they will have become human, and they will teach through the enlightened law of love. They will have learned to master their own desire, to calm their own storm. The law of love curtails the freedom of none, for it respects the free will of all. Those who live by it do not seduce their students, or allow themselves to be seduced by them. Some other teachers do. Usually, this is not with malicious intent, but because they are not strong enough to hold your trust, or kind enough to put your best interests before their own.

SIGNS OF A TRUSTWORTHY TEACHER

A trustworthy teacher will attempt to keep all relationships with others pure and honest. This means that they will not attempt to influence your energy, and they will not need to feel supported or fed by it. They will have a good supply of their own energy, through their heart's light, and will not need to feed off yours. They will not attempt to hook you energetically, and they will gently remove any hooks that you send out to them. The link that connects you to them will be crystal clear. You will feel strengthened and refreshed by it, for it is a chain of light and not a bind of need.

TRANSFERENCE IN HELPING RELATIONSHIPS

A competent teacher will be aware of the transference potential of any helping relationship, and will understand how to hold this transference, in order to give it back to you, when you have grown strong enough to take it. They will not use the transference dynamic as an excuse for the disempowerment and seduction of their students. This can happen when boundaries are blurred, and when the teacher is perceived by the student as one who can do everything for them.

This dependant dynamic is common in any form of guidance, but a true guide will never encourage it, although they will understand it. They will respect the free will of their students, and revere each person's unique soul. They will understand that to teach and guide others is a sacred responsibility, and that it carries a sacred trust. It is difficult to hold someone else's trust, if you cannot hold your own.

BEING RESPONSIBLE FOR YOUR ENERGETIC IMPACT ON OTHERS

As a student you may be attracted to a teacher, feeling that they have much to teach you. You may want to feel accepted and befriended by them. As you get closer to your teacher you may find that your energy is affected by theirs. The influence of the teacher's energy on your lower chakras (energy centres) may create in you feelings of urgent desire.

It is important that the teacher has moved through key areas in their own development, and thoroughly healed and balanced their own lower energy centres before they start to teach. Then the exchange of energy with their students can take place on a human level, that is at the level of the heart. If, however, they have not transformed their being by becoming human, they may be unaware of their own areas of weakness. Becoming responsible and trustworthy involves becoming responsible for your energetic effect on others, and ensuring that the impact of your energy does not disempower anyone else.

ETHERIC SEDUCTION

The teacher may also use their experience of the etheric level to seduce the student's etheric body. This is a form of abuse, as students may not fully understand what is going on, and probably will not have the vocabulary or the confidence to ask about it openly. A true initiation into a deeper spiritual path is always through the heart. Other kinds of initiation may interest you, but be aware of what they offer, and what they do not. They will not help you to share a human light or become trustworthy. Teachers that initiate you in this way have not completed a human path themselves. They will be spiritually weak, for the strong in spirit never use their knowledge and power to dominate the young. An evolved teacher will always respect your free will. They will teach you how to become truly strong, and how to discover the deeper levels of your being through the illumination of the heart.

SURVIVING THE STORM

If as a student you lack experience and discrimination, you may be swept along by the storm of desire, and enter into a sexual relationship with a teacher at this point. You will hopefully survive the storm and swim through it, but not everybody does. You can drown here, or remain stranded for years on the lonely island of an abusive relationship rooted in a power imbalance. You may eventually grow through this experience to understand what lay behind it, which was not love.

If you recognise what is happening, you are more likely to turn away: because what is happening has nothing to do with love, guidance or friendship. It has much to do with unmet need, displaced attachments, transferred longings, and often with issues of power and control. Sometimes people are attracted to positions of authority in which others come to them for guidance, because they need to feel in control over others to feel good about themselves. They may use their spiritual knowledge to manipulate the sexuality and emotions of others. Underneath, such teachers often have unresolved issues concerning their own adequacy and self worth. The emotion they feel towards their disciples or students is not a love that heals, but a distortion of love, a twisted love that rests on a power imbalance.

THE EFFECTS OF THE SICKNESS OF SELFISH DESIRE

In the end lust leads to loneliness and boredom, and twisted relationships cripple your heart's growth. Selfish desire takes you in the circle of the storm, and leads you nowhere; games of power lead you round and round and never bring you peace. Alone in the storm, confused by games of power, you lose your way.

The weed of lust grows quickly, strangling the wild flowers that sprouted with the sincere aspirations of your youth. The playfulness and joy you once felt in living will disappear, and you will become cynical and restless. Your spiritual path will become a charade behind which you learn to imitate your teacher, playing futile games of power. You will learn to flatter and seduce, to calculate the effect of your words and actions, to become insincere. Nothing will have lasting value for you. Long-term relationships will become difficult to sustain, because you will have lost the ability to care deeply, or to trust.

A CONSUMER MENTALITY

Using people corrupts your heart because it prevents you from deeply caring and trusting. You are caught in a circle going nowhere, far from faith and hope. This circle is one that consumes, and you embrace its energy, as you become a restless consumer of people and things. You are caught in a using mentality, a consumer mentality. This mentality is about buying and selling, using and being used. It is a mentality that makes us less than human, beings driven by lust and greed. There is no room in it for love or trust. The way out of the storm, the way out of a consumer mentality, is through compassion. As you learn the value of this compassion, you find something you can trust. You can then learn to trust and care for another, as you see them with the eyes of compassionate love. Until you do, it is difficult to stop using them carelessly.

THE VALUE OF BEING HUMAN

Until you realise the value of your humanity, nothing that you teach or learn will have lasting value. You will be teaching or learning how to consume, to consume knowledge, to consume ideas and to consume people. You will not be teaching or learning how to evaluate knowledge, or how to evaluate the true worth of human love and friendship. Until you discover your true value, and the true value of your relationships, you cannot evolve beyond a state of selfishness and confusion. To become a trustworthy human being is a real achievement, and until you realise this, not much is valuable.

To value another person's life is to turn your relationships from twisted transactions into a true sharing. Through deeply caring for another being, through respecting and honouring their life, and having your life respected and honoured by them, you learn to treasure another. This love helps to transform the lust in you that treats others as objects. Your own compassionate light teaches you the true value of human intimacy.

When you connect intimately with a partner through love and gratitude for their life, you bless them and they bless you, and your union is a sacred avenue to joy and grace. It is a sacrament that is valuable, for it holds within it the trust of two made one. Such a union enhances and adorns your humanity, just as the connection of lust and futile games of power debase it.

FINDING A POINT OF PERMANENT CALM
Any path that leads you into the storm will not bring you to grace. You cannot joyfully connect to life when you are in the storm, because you no longer connect to the vibration of love that embraces and nurtures life. You are connecting to a different vibration: one that goes on an endless round of consumption, and never reaches a point of permanent calm. To find permanent calm, the calm of real tranquillity, you must transcend this circle, as you transform your energy.

One way to transform your energy is through the medium of a loving relationship, or a loving friendship. In such a relationship, or friendship, you honour and revere another person's life. Through this attitude of reverence you are able to see the truth in each other, behind the veils of negativity and fear. By having faith in another person's essential grace, you are helped to find your own. Seeing this beauty in a partner or a friend, you learn to have faith in them, and to trust them. Together you learn to be human, as you share a compassionate light.

TURNING FROM THOSE WHO HAVE ABUSED YOUR TRUST

Teachers who use their students have ceased to be worthy of trust, for they have ceased to offer the trust of true friendship to the young. If you are fully human, you cannot manipulate others in this way, because you value them, and respect their free will. You cannot connect sexually without love, as you recognise the beauty of all life, and you cannot use it without love and care.

Recognise that one who would use you is not really your friend, that they have not yet found their own calm, and cannot yet trust themselves. Turn away from those who would use you carelessly, understanding that they still have much to learn, and that from them you have learned to see through the storm.

Turn your heart to all life, and find again the tune that makes you human. Know that without trust there is no true caring, and until you have calmed your own storm, you cannot trust yourself. Everyone who gets this far on their spiritual path, will have to encounter their storm, understand it, and learn how to calm it. In so doing they become safe havens for others, caught in the storm of selfish desire. They are able to teach by their being that there is another way to be.

THE MEDICINE FOR A SELFISH SPIRIT

The light of a compassionate heart is the only light that is stronger than the fire of selfish desire, the fire of lust. The fire of lust is fast and furious, and those without spiritual experience are immediately caught up in its flames. Those who are older, wiser, and stronger, do not fear this fire in themselves or others. Through concentrating on the light in the heart, they elevate their energy to a level beyond that of selfish desire. The light they radiate then calms the fire of others. The medicine that heals a selfish spirit is the steady influence of the light of the Christ within the heart. This light calms the storm of lust, as it bids the waves be still.

Do not be ashamed if you have been taken by the storm, and burned by the fire. It is by going through this experience that you have learned that it is possible to go beyond it. You can now learn to stand in the fire without getting burned as you calm the waves of your inner sea. Compassionate love will make you pure and strong, and able to help others who would otherwise drown.

BECOMING A TRUSTWORTHY TEACHER

For teachers who are slaves to their own desire, healing comes through having the courage to admit their error, their vulnerability and need, and their responsibility for those whose lives they may have damaged. The further you have strayed from a human path, the harder it is to return. For many it is too big a step to take, but those who do take it become an inspiration to others. To make amends for having used others, and to admit you are not fit to teach, brings healing, because you are forgiven by all of those true teachers who calmed the storm before you. They can help you find another way to be, and another way to teach. Through their forgiveness you are helped to make amends, and inspired to become a true teacher, one who can be trusted.

YOUR SPIRITUAL POWER

Tranquillity comes when you have calmed the storm and understood your own spiritual power. This is the power of the light within, that can calm any storm. You become fearless and free, as you learn to trust this light to protect you and guide you safely home. Your spiritual power also comes from your growing ability to discriminate and evaluate with wisdom. Your discrimination enables you to turn away from any situation that jeopardises your peace. None of us are victims unless we let ourselves be. Even as a young aspirant you have the power to refuse to be misled by a false teacher. The light of your heart will be able to discern their true worth. Trust the tuning fork of the heart, and decide whether their note is false or true. If it is false, turn from such teachers and follow your own true note.

FINDING YOUR STRENGTH

To be in control of your desires is to be in control of your own responses, your own decisions and ultimately your own life. You become strong as you learn to recognise patterns of relating that are unhealthy, and realise that you have the power to transform or to leave any relationship you are in that is not grounded in love and trust. You become strong as you realise that you can trust yourself, and that you know your own limits. By becoming one who spreads the light of trust, you become one who loves and cares compassionately, for love's sake, not your own. Until you have mastered your selfish desire you cannot trust yourself to respond with pure compassion to the longings and needs of others.

THE STEP OF TRANQUILLITY

To reach tranquillity your heart has to grow in strength and kindness. We discover our true value and our true power through the heart, through loving and being loved. The lesson of the fire and the storm is that only in a pure heart can we find peace, a heart that loves with compassion, that loves its brother as itself.

The step of tranquillity is difficult to reach. As you reach it the storm outside dies down, and a rosy light once more pervades the tower. You rest exhausted under the window of tranquillity. Light from this window has helped you find a precious calm, a serene grace. With tears you receive its beam, as you recognise its worth.

The next step on the tower of grace is courage. The step of courage is one you take when you have become tranquil through your own purity of heart. Before this you are not spiritually strong enough to be brave. You approach this step from the harbour of tranquillity, having learned how to master the fire and calm the storm.

THE WINDOW OF COURAGE

The light from the window of courage shines upon the traveller as they step towards truth. Real courage is not measured by outer displays of valour, but through your capacity to be true to yourself and others. You can only be true when you are functioning as a whole, not as a person with many different sides. If you lose your integrity you lose your courage, because real confidence is rooted in feeling at one with yourself. Losing your wholeness, your integrity, leaves you feeling weak, uncertain, and unsure of the truth. The light of courage is one that helps you become whole. Until you are, you cannot carry with confidence a human trust.

In the example below I will look at how you can lose your way, as you lose your integrity. I will then look at how you can find it again, as you find your courage.

THE SPIRITUAL SICKNESS OF DISHONESTY

Imagine that one day you have to make a choice between honesty and dishonesty. You may be offered a large sum of money, or promised a career opportunity, if you lie. You may be threatened or intimidated by others who want your support in a dishonest undertaking. You may be expected to keep silent, when you know you should speak out against something that is wrong. You may be asked to lie to cover up someone else's lies. You may be tempted to lie to save yourself from embarrassment; you may think that lying will make your life easier.

If you agree to lie, whatever the reason, you gradually lose your integrity, and with it your courage. When your integrity no longer holds you together, you start living in a dispersed state; you become uncertain, you lack inner strength. In this state you are essentially untrustworthy, as you are too weak to carry any kind of trust, and you cannot keep your word.

EFFECTS OF THE SICKNESS OF DISHONESTY

Even though the initial act of dishonesty may have been small, its effect on your inner being is damaging. The effect of any lie is to shatter your integrity, and weaken your conscience. If you listen to your conscience and act upon it, the mirror of your heart stays bright and clear. If you ignore your conscience, your heart loses its clarity and starts to cloud. This is why every act of untruth is important, as each one leads you to lose the brightness of the mirror that reflects your inner light. The more dishonest you become, the easier it is to live with deceit, and the further you stray from your own truth. Without integrity you have no centre. You have nothing solid on which to build your life. Without a pure heart or a clear conscience, you lose your direction, your integrity, and your strength.

RECOVERING YOUR SPIRITUAL HEALTH

The only way to become strong again is to choose not to lie. People sometimes experience serious illness or circumstantial chaos before they realise that a life without honesty will weaken them and make them ill. To recover your honesty and integrity is to recover your spiritual health. Until you stop lying you cannot be whole, you cannot be well, and you cannot be strong. Choosing truth comes as a relief, no matter what the consequences, because you find your centre again. Your strength returns as the split of deceit within you heals; not having to deceive yourself, or others, means that you can become whole again.

THE VALUE OF INTEGRITY

Nobody can take your integrity away from you, even if they kill you, but you can give it away at any time. You give it away every time you lie, or support a lie. A person who values their truth accepts death more easily than he or she can accept a life based on lying. Understanding the value of your integrity is understanding the value of your life. How much is it worth to be true? How much is your life worth if you are not? These are the questions that are asked by those who stand upon the threshold of a human circle. They are questions that cannot be avoided when you reach a certain stage on your path.

THE STEP OF COURAGE

You will not be called upon to ask yourself such questions until your soul is old enough to answer them. When it is you will have to answer them alone, for this is how true courage is born in the soul. To take this step you have to have discovered for yourself the value of your own truth. You have to know that it is worth dying for, that this is what makes it worth living for. The step of courage is a step towards spiritual maturity, an initiation into adulthood, that those on a true spiritual path must take alone. When you have taken this step, you will feel the strength of an army behind you. This army was always there, but you didn't know it. This is the army of all of those who took this step before.

FREEDOM FROM HIERARCHIES OF FEAR

Hierarchies of fear exist when people are afraid to tell the truth. When you fear death less than lying, no hierarchy of any kind can intimidate you. The step towards truth is a step you take as you become honest, brave and strong. As you take it you leave behind the cowardice of the vicious, and discover what it is that makes you truly brave. Only a human being can see beyond the instinct for self-preservation that engenders fear. Only a human being can remain true to a principle that is worth more to them than their physical existence. Only a human being can be conscious and fearless enough to make this choice, for only a human being can be guided by the compassionate light of the heart. This light is truer than the dominion of fear, for it lasts beyond and before our physical existence in matter.

The light of compassion enlightens our evolutionary path, and helps us see our true worth. As we leave behind the way of fear we understand that this light embodies our truth, and that is why it is worth dying for. For without it our existence is illusory, and our way is never clear.

THE WHITE LILY OF TRUTH

It doesn't matter if your choice for truth is small and insignificant, in comparison to others. No matter how small your step, if you stand alone for truth you will discover the courage of the spiritually strong. As you do a white lily will bloom on this step, as the light of courage illumines the way ahead. The lily of truth blooms on your path as you become brave enough to hold a human trust. It is a symbol of the integrity and purity of truth for which you now stand, and for which others also stood. It matters little if no one else knows about your inner choice for truth. The others in this circle know, and in spirit they now stand beside you. Together you stand for the integrity of the truth, that is stronger than armies and the whole machinery of lies that uphold all hierarchies of fear. No amount of force can take the truth away from you, or split the united strength of this brave company.

Once you have felt the strength of the truth, and its torchbearers, you cease to fear the power of lies. You become one who can welcome others into the circle of the brave. You become one who can share your courage and integrity with others, who are in need of your strength. Though you may be only one, you are stronger than the multitude who lack courage.

THE MEDICINE FOR A WEAK SPIRIT

The medicine for a weak spirit is found in respect for truth. Becoming more honest will help you to become brave. For the truth gives you back the courage you lost when you broke your trust. Without trust in the truth and its healing power, none of us can be brave and strong.

If you want to become more honest in your life, but do not see any dramatic choices that you have to make, you can become stronger through respecting the truth in small ways. You can chose to be more honest in your relationships. You can choose to understand the value of your own integrity, and not to give it away.

It takes courage to follow a compassionate path in a consumer age. It takes courage to be human, when few value this goal. The fact that you are trying in your own small way to be a human being of integrity will have an effect on those around you. Light from this window will help you befriend others who are scared of being true, who are frightened into lying. You will become a source of strength to those still tangled up in lies, who have lost their integrity, not realising it's worth. Part of your integrity will come from your willingness to share your understanding, as you support those who are confused, uncertain, and unsure of what being human means.

TEACHERS WHO LACK COURAGE

Do not evaluate your teachers by how much they know, or how much they can do. Evaluate them on their courage and their integrity. If they are not honest and brave, know that nothing they can teach you will make you spiritually strong. If you find no brave elders, do not trust anyone to lead you, except your own inner light. This is the light that transcends all hierarchies of fear, the light that leads to grace. Let your inner light be your guide, and it will lead you to the step of courage.

THE TIMELESS CIRCLE OF THE BRAVE

As you become an adult on a human path, you leave behind the shallowness of your time, and join the timeless circle of the brave. A company of fearless souls become your spiritual companions as you take this step. If no one is willing to take this step, humanity loses its way, as there are none brave enough to hold the torch of trust in a dark age. For this reason there have been individuals in every time, who stood for the truth, in defiance of all hierarchies of fear. They held the torch and would not let it fall, they were trustworthy unto death. Through their courage they kept a human path alight for those behind them. You now hold this torch for all of those who will climb the stair behind you.

From now on every time you need spiritual strength, you can call on the support of this circle. As you grow spiritually, your network of spiritual support increases. A strong source of support comes from those who lit the ages past, with the torch of their humanity and love. It is their spiritual strength you receive on this step.

Understanding your debt to all of those who went before you, and your responsibility to all of those behind you, you are ready to rise to the next step. As you approach it the light falling through the windows in the tower changes colour, from rosy pink to red. Before you and behind you on the staircase a tumult has arisen. Shadowy forms are fighting on the step above you, others are shouting at each other on the stairs below. Here before the last step of this stair, you find yourself on a battlefield, surrounded by shadowy demons.

THE STEP OF PATIENCE

The step of patience is the hardest step of all to take. As you approach it, you will encounter all of your inner demons once again, the ones you thought you left behind on the steps below.

You will meet again the face of your pride, your lust, your greed, your cowardice, and your deceit. These qualities never die in you, they just become weaker as you become spiritually strong. You approach this step as the red dawn illumines the way ahead. Here you will meet your demons once more, and reconcile them as you master them, with the help of the light of patience.

THE WINDOW OF PATIENCE

In the alchemy of the heart, patience is the philosopher's stone, the vital ingredient that changes the base metal of your being into gold. In the tower of grace you may try for years, without success, to take the step of patience. No true path is without this step, one of the hardest to take, and one of the most blessed.

Patience is an underrated quality today, where much rests on speed. Even on the spiritual path people want quick or even instant transformation. To transform is to grow into something different, and in spiritual terms this is a gradual process. By the time you have reached the step of patience you will have already been on a path for many years, and will understand something of your own nature. The step of patience involves a gradual change, a change that transforms both your inner and outer being.

LOSING CLEAR SIGHT AS YOU LOSE PATIENCE

When you lose patience you lose your ability to see clearly; what you want, and what you want to do, become uppermost in your mind. You lose patience when you are thwarted in the desires of your will. When your will loses patience beyond a certain degree you are roused to anger. Most anger is a reaction to a lack of patience, and clearly shows that you have lost clear sight. Without clear sight you cannot trust yourself.

ANGER THAT IS JUST

The anger that is not a reaction to this lack is of a different order, it is the anger of the just whose power protects. Such anger is roused by injustice and cruelty, and serves a useful purpose: it frightens away the predators who prey on the vulnerable. It is the kind of power that protects children and vulnerable adults from exploitation and abuse. To be able to express this kind of anger usefully you need to be without self-interest. In this case your anger is pure, and safeguards the weak by frightening away those who would cause them harm. It does not seek retribution or revenge, it seeks to protect. Such anger is rare however; most of our anger is the other kind.

THE SPIRITUAL SICKNESS OF RAGE

There is a quality that lurks beneath the surface of the self, that you may not yet have recognised. This is the angry red demon of your rage. We all have one, but whether you recognise him, depends upon your level of self-knowledge. (Your demon may be male or female, they are not necessarily male.) If you doubt that you have an angry demon within, ask someone to observe you next time you are in a rage. He usually pops out, and you look quite different. You may stamp your feet, clench your fists and change colour. You are in his grip, you cannot say he is in yours. He can do much damage, damage that you never meant to inflict, but that he does. He can make you hit your spouse, your child or your friend, he can incite you to murder. In your anger you lose clear sight and clear understanding; all is forgotten in a moment of blind rage. Your anger renders you out of control, so that you no longer know what you are doing, or where you are going. In this state you cannot trust yourself, or hold anyone else's trust.

ANGER TURNED INWARD

You may say that you are never violent, never even angry, but this does not mean that your demon is not hiding within you. He may have been pushed down, well out of harm's way, but he's still there. People who become passive often turn their anger inward, and then their demon makes them ill. He causes them to feel angry with themselves, to sabotage their potential. Whether he is expressed or repressed, the little red demon will always cause you pain. You are not in control of yourself until he stops hurting both you and other people.

UNDERSTANDING YOUR RAGE

Understanding your anger and your tendency to rage or self-hatred, is necessary, you need to know your demon. By getting to know him, you begin to learn what motivates and moves him. He doesn't like to be crossed, he likes his own way at all times. He doesn't like to listen, he likes to lead. He doesn't like gentleness, or humour or kindness, they irritate him. He likes to be in control, and to silence others. All of us have the same demon, he is not unique. In all of us lie the seeds of his tyranny, but luckily most of us never get a chance to let them grow into the bitter harvest of anger's sons.

THE SPIRITUAL SICKNESS OF AN AGE WITHOUT PATIENCE

Anger's sons are those who have lost all humanity. They only know how to ravage, maim and kill. We should not blame too harshly those who become anger's sons, and commit acts of atrocity in war. We did not teach them to know their own demon. We gave them no weapons of wisdom, patience and compassion to resist the onslaught of his murderous rage; no antidote to protect them from the contagious fever of his insanity. We did not teach them the first lesson of their humanity, which is a profound respect for all life.

This harvest will go on, with each new generation infected by its bitterness, until we teach our young to be human. Only then can we begin to heal the spiritual sickness that affects an age without patience. This is the harvest of the red demon who knows no love and shows no mercy. It is the viciousness of the jungle unleashed in a frenzy of blood. Not until we as a race become fully human will this destructive capacity be left behind, as it ceases to serve us. Until then we cannot call ourselves a human race at all, for we are often less than human, and unable to hold any kind of trust.

THE REFINEMENT OF THE WILL

We are all responsible for the collective havoc wreaked by the red demon and his sons, until we recognise his little accomplice in ourselves. By getting to know your demon, you begin to understand him. You begin to understand the root of your viciousness. The root of your anger and rage is your selfish will, which always wants its own way. We all live in a state of conflict, but this conflict is resolved neither by getting your own way, nor by surrendering your will to someone else. This conflict is resolved by refining your will, as it becomes the servant of your inner light. This resolution is achieved through patience. For your little demon cannot understand love or gentleness, and he cannot be taught by either; but he can be taught by patience.

THE MEDICINE FOR AN ANGRY SPIRIT

As you get to know yourself you will begin to recognise when your angry demon is about to appear. At this point ask for patience. Patience will help you see beyond the situation that angers you, that renders you out of control. As you see beyond your anger, take the assistance that patience offers you. The medicine of patience is a golden chain. It is a chain that you slip around your demon's neck; it doesn't hurt him, but it restricts his movement. This is not the collar of repression that is another form of violence, but the restraint of wisdom, which brings peace. The peace hidden in patience comes as through the restraining hand of wisdom your rebellious lower soul becomes obedient. It becomes obedient not to the command of another, but to the wise dominion of your heart's pure light.

THE STEADINESS OF THE TRULY STRONG

Until you become patient and obedient to your inner light, you will not be truly strong, no matter how brave you are. You will not have discovered the steadiness of the truly strong who oppress no one, and who are not oppressed by anyone. Patience gives you this equilibrium, this steady strength. It teaches you forbearance, which is the ability to calm your anger through the light of mercy. It uncovers this light within your heart, a light that refines and ennobles the human soul.

THE LIGHT OF MERCY

Your demon never goes away, but he becomes obedient, tamed by patience and calmed by a merciful light. The light of mercy teaches him forgiveness, tolerance and respect for life. As your demon learns, your soul is ennobled. A noble soul is a soul that chooses mercy over vengeance, and kindness over cruelty. It has transcended a purely self-centred outlook, and cares about the welfare of the whole. A noble soul is ashamed of its own capacity for harm, and has decided the price of further rebellion is too high. For this reason it submits its will to the restraining chain of patience, and the refining light of mercy.

Through such a process you learn to be gentle with yourself and others, as the desire of your will to dominate, possess and destroy is gradually transformed. Love for all life renders you patient and pure, as you come to experience the trust of brotherhood. Through the mastery of patience your demon is tamed, and becomes a child ready to learn. He no longer wants to harm you or anyone else, for he has discovered a more satisfying way to be.

A TEST OF PATIENCE

If you really want to progress in patience, choose to be with people who test your good will. Choose to spend time with those who try your patience, with difficult individuals, with the querulous sick, the annoying child, the boring relative. Then judge for yourself your own level of spiritual attainment. The more sincerely patient, gentle and kind you are, the further you have progressed. The more irritated and angry you become, the more you have to learn.

This is a much more reliable test of your spiritual level than any other kind of appraisal, because it's one you cannot hide behind. If you want to progress more quickly, in order to become a trustworthy human being, then choose to be patient every day. Choose to be patient with people, with circumstances, with situations when you don't get your own way, with yourself. Stop rushing and take a long-term view. Accept the sovereignty of the heart, as you train your will with the sweet chain of patience. Patience is sweet because it purifies all that it touches, just as the light of mercy softens the most callous heart. Encourage the alchemy of the heart, seek the transformative power of patience. This is the way to clarify your sight, to purify your heart, and to ennoble your soul.

THE TRUE TEACHER IN THE CLASSROOM OF THE HEART

As you become more patient you radiate an energy that cools the anger of others; you become a soothing presence. Because your demon is calm, he cannot be roused by theirs, but serves to calm theirs down. If you have no patience your energy does the opposite, as their demon incites yours, and off you both go into the fray. Becoming patient means that you have a lot less to fear. You fear the anger of others less, because you have calmed your own.

Anger is not the only demon that patience can tame. As your angry demon becomes calm, you realise that patience is the true teacher in the classroom of the heart. Patience takes the sting out of your pride and arrogance, and bridles your selfish desire.

Patience is a true friend of courage, as it enables you to endure and persevere. Deceit flees from patience, as patience sees through quick-tempered lies. Desire and ambition are always impatient, demanding immediate fulfilment. Patience robs them both of their power. Patience is the crown of the virtues, for through it all the others are made strong. Without patience, none of them can last. However kind, brave, honest and calm you are, without patience you cannot carry a lasting trust.

BECOMING MASTER OF YOURSELF

As the light of mercy shines in your heart, the window of patience opens above you, and the tower of grace is filled with a clear light. The demons on the stair before you become still. Those that fought above you, and those that yelled behind you, become quiet and calm. The light of patience illumines your path, as you leave behind the blindness of the vicious forever. As you take this step, the demons in the tower kneel before you with heads bowed. You have become the master of yourself.

You are now strong enough to hold a human trust through every storm, strong enough to be true through every circumstance. You have taken a big step on your personal journey, and in your own small way have contributed to the collective evolution of your kind.

THE CHAIN OF HUMANITY

As you leave behind all traces of a vicious way of being, you recognise the treasure you hold in your heart, the jewel that has transformed you and made you strong. Through the attainment of patience your breast is adorned with a stone of grace. This stone hangs upon a golden chain. This is the same chain that helped you restrain your demon that he might learn, the chain that made your heart a source of mercy and of calm. You wear it with humility, knowing the years you took to earn it, knowing that your anger did much harm. This is the chain of the viceregency of Adam and Eve, the chain of humanity you earn as you become a trustworthy human being. Until you have mastered yourself you cannot care for creation with compassion and tenderness. Until you earn the chain of trust, you cannot reclaim the place that Adam lost. Your place in creation is to be the mirror of the Divine. This is why patience is the key to joy, for it is the stone that reclaims your grace, as it reclaims your trust.

PATHS WITHOUT PATIENCE
Those whose path does not include the step of patience fall further from grace as they increase their knowledge and power. They are quick to anger, and slow to forgive. A self-interested teacher with occult power may use their power to harm those who anger them, and thus their students will fear incurring their wrath. Not being patient, such a teacher cannot teach patience, and their restlessness will take root in the hearts of their students, who will lack patience also. They will learn to be like their teacher, to command respect through fear.

Only a patient teacher can teach the true lesson of this realm, the lesson of our humanity. The truly patient condemn no one, and accept the most vicious as their students. This is because they have the patience to tolerate them, and the strength of spirit to be able to train them. Having trained and refined their own will, they can gently yet firmly refine the rebellious will of the most wild. A true guide fears no-one, for they are protected by their own light. If you learn to love your enemies you disempower even the most misguided; for no power is stronger than the power of love. Those who have become truly brave and patient trust this power. They teach with patience, and through their wisdom and compassion they help the most dangerous find another way to be.

BECOMING SPIRITUALLY WELL
If on your spiritual path you attempt to bypass the stair of kindness, in order to progress more quickly, you will not flourish. Your pride, your vanity, your lust, your greed, your dishonesty, your cowardice or your anger will eventually make you ill. The stair of kindness is one on which you become spiritually well, so that you can be of service to the rest of your kind. To be a human being is to be kind, to be humble, to be generous, to be truthful, to be brave, to be patient. This is how we are born to be, but most of us were not educated properly, these qualities were not fostered in us and allowed to grow. We were not taught how to heal ourselves and

become whole. On the stair of kindness we relearn the lessons of our humanity, and heal the sicknesses in our nature that hinder us from further spiritual growth.

THE GARDEN OF A PURE HEART

After the step of patience you have graduated from the school of the heart. Having progressed this far you can be trusted to uphold the qualities that humanise and ennoble the human race. Your heart has become a garden, where others may find rest. The flowers in the garden of a pure heart are those you tended, through the years of spiritual struggle. They include the sweet vine of kindness, the wild flowers of tranquillity, and the lily of truth, the flower of the brave.

Your spiritual training in this lifetime may end here. On the stair of kindness your heart has been purified, and your nature transformed. You have learned that which you need to know to be a healing presence in the world, and you have become permanently trustworthy. Through your being you are able to teach others how to be human, and how to hold a human trust.

THE NEXT LEVEL OF SPIRITUAL DEVELOPMENT

If you so wish however, you can choose to continue your path. From the step of patience you can rise to the next level of spiritual development, the level that can only be safely attained by those who have become fully trustworthy. Because of their spiritual and human integrity they will not misuse the knowledge that they gain on the next stage of the way. You will now enter the university of spiritual purity, a school for the mature, where your soul will be purified and transformed.

THE STAIR OF PURITY

In the tower of grace you have reached a new stage. On the stair of kindness you walked into the daylight, and found a warmer, kinder world. On the stair of purity you will enter a world of beauty. The windows on the stair above are different from the ones you passed before; the panes of each one are inlaid with precious stones. As the sun passes through them the jewels catch the sunlight and colours dance on the steps below.

On this stair your life will become a jewel that you polish day by day, as your path becomes a prayer. Although this part of your journey is not without difficulty, the beauty of the windows ahead will entrance you, so that often you will not notice your own effort. The steps ahead are for lovers, lovers of truth, whose vocation in life lies in the realm of the spirit. That which you will learn on this stair will harmonise, uplift and transform you, so that eventually you may leave all steps behind, and soar upwards through the domes of grace.

THE STAIR OF
PURITY

4

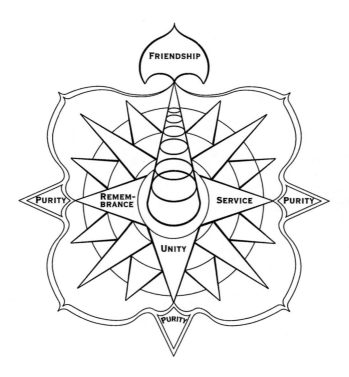

The Diamond Window of Purity
❖
The Ruby Window of Remembrance
❖
The Sapphire Window of Service
❖
The Emerald Window of Unity

THE STAIR OF PURITY

**Where the soul is purified through
remembrance and service, and
transformed through unity**

To reach the stair of purity you will have passed
through the stages of faith, hope, and kindness,
and achieved a measure of inner and outer spiritual
maturity. At this point you have become a
trustworthy human being, one who can be relied on
to act with integrity and compassion.

Those who travel further are those who have a
spiritual vocation. The windows on this stair are
jewelled, inlaid with diamonds, rubies, sapphires,
and emeralds. These gems reflect the increasing
spiritual beauty uncovered in the heart of the
aspirant as he or she travels through the higher
stages of the way.

On this stage of the journey your soul is purified
and transformed. You learn how to concentrate
your attention through remembrance, and how to
dedicate your life through service. You learn to
experience the truth of unity, which involves losing
all limitation, as you lose the idea of your limited
self. Once the unity of being has been experienced
you are free from the limitations of your
perception and conditioning, and can understand
the oneness of the Divine that encompasses all
things. At this point you are able to share the cup
of unity, love and knowledge which through your
spiritual effort you have earned.

THE DIAMOND WINDOW OF PURITY

The traveller now stands on the threshold of the stair of purity. Rays of coloured light fall onto the steps below, from the jewelled windows above. The first window on this stair is the diamond window of purity. Pure diamonds cast rainbows of light upon this step, as inwardly the traveller's soul becomes pure and true.

The step of purity is one you take when you are ready to evolve to a new level of being. It is a step that involves a change in your lifestyle, your outlook and your energy.

A CHANGE IN LIFESTYLE

As you grow spiritually your lifestyle often changes. You grow out of one way of being into another that better reflects your new understanding. Such change is an individual process, and there are few general guidelines. You may find that you need to change your occupation, to do what you feel called to do. You may change the way you relate to those close to you. You may find that your diet changes, that you want to eat a purer, lighter diet. You may feel an urge to give up long standing habits, such as smoking or drinking alcohol. None of these changes are necessary for spiritual growth. However, they may happen naturally, for as you evolve and change so does your lifestyle.

If you attempt to change your lifestyle, but still have a self-centred outlook, then such change may not help you. If you have not learned to know yourself, you can hide behind a 'spiritual' lifestyle while making little real progress. Becoming pure in a spiritual sense is not about fasting, eating a vegetarian diet, meditating regularly, working in healing or leaving behind materialistic values. Becoming spiritually pure involves learning to love others with a pure unselfish love. It involves learning to forgive, as you begin to see clearly. If you concentrate too much on yourself and your lifestyle, you may become driven and self-obsessed. If you concentrate on becoming more patient and tolerant your life will change in a relaxed and natural way. It is a good idea to concentrate on the positive qualities of the heart at the same time, or before, you attempt to change your way of life.

A CHANGE IN OUTLOOK
As well as a change in lifestyle, the step of purity often involves a change in outlook. The outlook that evolves as you become more pure, is an outlook of greater tolerance. However, while you become more tolerant and understanding of others, the work you have done on the steps below has given you a new perspective on yourself. On this step you understand that certain ethical guidelines will influence your future spiritual progress and your life.

ETHICAL GUIDELINES
One reason you need such guidelines at this stage, is that other people may come to you looking for advice and guidance. Although you are not yet ready to be a spiritual guide, there will be people whom you can help, just as there are people who can help you. It is important that your own ethics are clear to you, and that they inform your outlook and your dealings with others. It is also important that you do not expect others to follow your ethical code. This tolerance and open-minded attitude towards others, coupled with a clear understanding of your own ethics, are a sign of your spiritual maturity.

Nobody else can tell you what your personal guidelines should be. You have to discover your own, the ones that are true for you. Here are mine, some of which may match yours:

1. Aim to be unselfish in your conduct with others.
2. Be honest.
3. Practice patience.
4. Try not to criticise other people or interfere with their affairs.
5. Do not seek recognition, and do not do things in order to receive it.
6. Forget your personal importance, and work for the healing of the whole.
7. Trust the power of unconditional love, the strongest power.

BECOMING SPIRITUALLY MATURE

Ethical guidelines help you to keep track of yourself and your own behaviour. You may be trustworthy, but you still need an ethical framework. That way when you meet other people who do not have one, you will not be influenced by them. You will know exactly what your boundaries are, and what you expect from yourself. Becoming pure involves having a clear direction, knowing where you are going and why. It means that your intentions and your actions become truer. It is also important that you do not have high expectations of others.

A change in outlook means that your motives become more pure, as you cease to have a self-orientated frame of reference. Although it may seem that your outlook changed earlier on the path, on the stairs of hope and kindness, it is on the stair of purity that your outlook becomes refined. This happens through a gradual process of understanding, as you see more clearly why we are here.

We are here to love one another, and to forgive each other and ourselves. On the stair of purity these aims become clearer, as they are translated into our inner and outer experience. It is through an ethical framework that you ensure that they are translated into congruent action. Most people need such a framework. It's one way you can help yourself to become more true, in intention and action. Such a framework helps you check yourself, thereby increasing your self-awareness. Without one it's easy to have blind spots, to criticise others while remaining unaware of your own inconsistencies.

A CHANGE IN ENERGY

As you become more pure and true, your energy changes. This involves a change in your vibratory level. We are made up of energy, and our subtle bodies vibrate at different rates. Your vibratory level influences your ability to transmit and receive communications on a subtle level.

The safest and easiest way to raise your vibratory level is through transforming the energy of your fear into the energy of love. Two steps towards a more loving way of being are remembrance and service, and they are described in the next two chapters. This transformation is also achieved through a change in attitude, and a change in motivation. As your aims become purer, so does your energy. As you become less selfish, so your energy becomes lighter and less dense. This is because the transformation of your consciousness affects your energetic blueprint. You are not the same now as you were when you started your path. Your outlook, your behaviour, your aspirations, your intentions and your priorities have changed; and this changes the nature of your energy.

PURSUING A PATH OF COMPASSIONATE LOVE

If you want to accelerate the rate of change of your vibratory level, actively pursue a path of compassionate love. See everyone you meet as a person who needs love, and understand your own need for it. See through the tangled behaviour of other people, to the fear of being unloved that lies behind it. See through your own fear; touch your own unloved self. Make every day an opportunity to love more. In this way your being will turn gracefully to love. Love is the highest rate of vibration, the highest frequency. It's one that everything alive responds to and needs. Our path is a process of returning to this frequency, for we are in essence the pure energy of love. If you want to evolve quickly, then evolve through love, and leave behind the disharmony of fear.

GROWTH IN SUBTLE AWARENESS

As your vibratory level changes, you may become more sensitive to the vibrations of other people, of places and of objects. You may also become aware of your own subtle bodies, and be able to detach your etheric body from your physical body at will. You may learn how to move around in your etheric body, while your physical body remains stationary. You may walk between the worlds, being able to move around at will on the etheric and other levels, which are lighter than this one.

You may learn to communicate with others through the telepathy of the heart; you may be able to communicate over long distances. You may become clairvoyant, clairaudient or clairsentient. You may be able to do all of the above, or none of them. None of them are important in themselves. What matters is that your being is becoming unified through love. Awareness of your subtle bodies is one way that your increasing purity of being may show itself.

But this awareness is not a proof of spiritual growth. Proof of this is an unselfish attitude of love and forgiveness towards other people, and a clarity of purpose regarding the goal of your path.

If you grow in subtle awareness there is always a danger that you will be distracted from your true goal, and end up for years playing around on the etheric level. Although such gifts as clairvoyance etc. can serve a useful purpose, they are not an end in themselves. They are signs that you have developed in certain areas, but they are not proof of true spiritual maturity, or true spiritual purity. So if you find yourself fascinated by your growth on subtle levels, be aware that you can waste much time here.

PATHS OF SELF-INTEREST AND THE ETHERIC LEVEL
Paths of self-interest use the etheric level as a means of increasing occult power. Mastery of this level means that you can use it to obtain what you want in the material world. You can use your knowledge of it to influence, seduce, manipulate or intimidate other people. Power games on the etheric level will not serve your evolutionary progress at all. If you meet powerful figures on this level who threaten your equilibrium, do not be afraid of them. Only your fear will give them any power over you. Ask for the assistance and protection of the Truth, and of the friends of Truth. If you ask for help you will always be guided and protected by friends from the unseen realm, who watch over the sincere aspirant who is pure of heart. The light of their protection is firm and strong. Do not be distracted by sorcerers, wizards, black magicians and the whole collection of individuals on this level, who may want to show you another way.

REMAINING TRUE TO YOUR ORIGINAL AIMS
Walk through the etheric market place and remain pure. Do not buy anything, and do not sell yourself. If you love the truth, you will pass through this level, and nothing will hold you here. You may develop many skills, but none of them will make you proud. You may hold power in your hands, but you will use it wisely. You will see through the paths of others, and know that their path may be right for them, but it is not for you. You will criticise no one, but you will not be deceived by them either. You will become a

wise innocent, secure in the power of love, as you trust the light of your heart to show you the way. In this manner you will be able to handle the transition into living on more than one level, and the increased vulnerability and strength that such a transition brings.

To reach the step of purity, you have to understand what is important in your own spiritual growth. Because you may advance quickly at this stage, you need to know what your priorities are. As your lifestyle, outlook and energy patterns change, so your priorities need to stay constant. The qualities that will help you reach this step are dedication, tolerance, clarity of intent, courage, and an unselfish attitude of love and forgiveness towards everyone. As long as your aims remain true you will not be thrown off by an accelerated rate of growth; you will draw closer to the goal.

THE JEWEL OF THE PURE

Climbing to the step of purity a diamond falls on your path from the window above you. The light of a pure diamond is the light of those who have learned much, but who are not seduced by their knowledge. It is for those who have cut through illusion, to find their own truth. It is for those who can be trusted with knowledge and power, who will not exploit, who will remain humble and pure of heart.

From the diamond window of purity a clear light descends on you. Through this light you see the next step on the tower of grace, the step of remembrance. On this step a crimson light is falling, from the rubies inlaid in the window above.

THE RUBY WINDOW OF REMEMBRANCE

THE JEWEL OF REMEMBRANCE

The window of remembrance shows you a different way to be. The way of remembrance is the way of the pure who are peaceful, and whose presence radiates peace. Remembrance is a jewel that you may be lucky enough to find if you are destined for the spiritual life. The ruby of your heart's remembrance turns silence to tranquillity, and idleness to reflection. Remembrance eases your progress, as it illumines your heart and purifies your spirit.

Spiritual practice, as mentioned earlier in this book, differs from person to person, and it is important to find a form that suits you. By now your spiritual practice will have illumined your heart to a certain degree. What matters at this stage is that your practice becomes something that constantly reminds you, something that you can return to all the time, not just at the time of meditation or prayer.

REMEMBRANCE OF A WORD OR PHRASE

Many people attempt to illumine their heart and become more peaceful, by remembering a word or phrase that they silently repeat through their breath, through the minutes and hours of each day. The word may be the name of a beloved friend and teacher such as Jesus, Buddha, or Krishna. It may be an attribute of God, such as in the Islamic tradition, where God is called upon through His Names (the Light, the One, the Eternal, etc.) the highest name encompassing all the others, being Allah. Some people prefer to repeat a word such as Love, Peace or Truth. Some may use a mantra, such as 'OM', where the sound of the word has within it a primordial resonance. The energy that you bring to any remembrance is more important than the word or phrase you use. The more love and devotion you give your remembrance, the better it will work.

REASONS FOR REMEMBRANCE

People have different reasons for choosing to repeat a word or phrase silently through the day. They may do so to calm their energy, to focus their wandering thoughts. They may do so in order to be mindful, to be more aware of the consequences of their words and actions. They may repeat a mantra because this is how they have been instructed to proceed on their spiritual path. They may remember in order to bring down the grace of the One remembered, to instill a more graceful energy into their daily lives. They may practice remembrance because they love the Truth. The more loving your motive, the more your practice will remind you of the love that you are.

A PATH OF DEVOTIONAL REMEMBRANCE
If the practice of devotional remembrance suits you, then choose a word, and repeat it silently through the day to yourself. Repeat it continuously, to the rhythm of your breath, whenever you can. You will find it becomes a long lost friend. There is great beauty and power in a path of devotional remembrance. The beauty comes from the transformation of your life that such concentration brings. The power comes from the strength of spirit that such attention gives you.

If you are whole hearted in your remembrance, it will become a refuge, a harbour in the storm of life. You will know how to find your own inner pool of peace, you will know how to contact and connect with a well spring of inner calm. Your practice will bring you strength, for through it you will acquire greater depth of being. When things go wrong, when you are upset by outer events in your life, you will be able to recover your equilibrium through the rhythm of your breath. Your life will become a melody of inner peace, no matter what the outer turbulence. You will also be able to achieve more outwardly than you did before; this is because you will be wasting less energy on anxiety or indecision.

THE INNER BEAUTY OF THE CONTEMPLATIVE LIFE
A way of remembrance is for those who love the truth, and if you are attracted to this way you will follow it, even if you do so alone. You may not belong to a spiritual order or community where remembrance is practiced daily. You may have left organisations and orders, finding that their teaching did not ring true. You may never have joined any formal organisation, or received any formal

spiritual training, as these did not suit the development of your own particular soul.

Whatever your background, a way of remembrance is possible for you, and you can practice remembrance in any sort of life. You do not have to live in the mountains, or in a monastery, to taste the inner beauty of the contemplative life. You can find it wherever you are, in a life that is boring and bleak, and full of repetitive menial work. If there is little space in your life for beauty or joy, you can find these things through the remembrance of the heart; a life that is outwardly grey can become an inner tapestry of light and grace. This is why remembrance is a jewel. Its transformative power enables your soul to experience the beauty that is locked within you. It is a path of silent beauty, a secret path for the pure of soul.

You need no formal instruction to follow this way, but you do need to feel an attraction to it, an attraction that will make you want to focus your attention. The longing of your heart and the aspiration of your breath are all that you need. A path of remembrance is one of longing and desire; it will not work if you force yourself to do it. If you do, you will feel tired, strained and disappointed. This way is not about results; it is about dissolving into a love that gradually envelops you.

OTHER WAYS TO MAKE YOUR LIFE A PRAYER
If a way of remembrance is not for you, you will feel no attraction to it. Don't worry if this is the case, your way may be more active, it may be more centred on service. It may be more celebratory; it may include dance and song. Find your own way, the way that your heart calls you to. There are many ways to make your life a prayer, many ways to turn to love. The way of remembrance is just one of them.

HELPERS ON A PATH OF REMEMBRANCE
Even though you may practice a path of remembrance on your own, there are many unseen helpers ready to assist you, if you need them. If you have made an inner commitment to a way of remembrance, you will be helped by those who followed such a way before, and who are now willing and eager to help others. The spirit of a teacher from the past may aid you, especially if you

follow a path of devotional remembrance in their name. Your own personal guide or guardian angel may help you. You may be assisted by a whole community of evolved souls no longer embodied, whose work on other levels is geared towards helping humanity evolve. This is the community of the White Brotherhood. This is the name that this community is known by, and it includes souls that were once embodied as men or women, and who lived in bodies of all different skin colours and racial groups. The White Brotherhood help anyone who asks them sincerely for assistance, and their help is always positive.

In every age there were some who wanted to serve the Light, and who chose to remember the Divine above all others. If you are one of them let nothing stand in the way of your true calling. Be faithful in your remembrance, and do not be discouraged. Be aware of the spiritual support of all those who went this way before you, and take strength from their strength. Their gift to you is the warmth of a companionship that outlives time and space. Such assistance will help you to centre yourself in remembrance, and to understand your spiritual purpose. A path of remembrance will bring you peace and joy. If it's what you are made for, follow it, inspired by the breath of all of those who went this way before.

ACCESS TO AN INNER TREASURY

As you begin to live in remembrance, your inner life will change. As your spirit drinks the still water of your inner remembrance you will experience a lightness of being, and a new sense of calm. Every true spiritual path has times of difficulty and doubt, for if it did not you would not learn how to be brave and strong. Moments of reflection and remembrance are the way that you discover your own inner treasury of peace, which cannot be lost, only obscured. Remembrance is the way you draw aside the veil from this inner treasury, and enter a secret chamber hidden deep within. It is the way you experience the sweetness of intimacy with the Divine. It is through your breath that this intimacy is sealed. Your breath is your life, and if you are in loving connection with every breath, then you share your life with every breath. Through such a process of dedicated remembrance your soul is refined and purified.

SPIRITUAL STATES

In the earlier stages of remembrance individuals may well experience the sweetness of spiritual states. These are states that steal upon you, often during times of remembrance and prayer. Their sweetness encourages people to continue in remembrance, but never seek such states, and do not try to recreate them. To remember so that you receive a gift is to love like a child. If you love like a bride, you will see through the gift, to the One who gives it.

PURIFICATION OF THE SOUL THROUGH DEVOTIONAL REMEMBRANCE

Conscious remembrance purifies you, so that your soul gradually becomes peaceful through the energy of love. It is a gentle transformation, and it will show in your face. You will lose your hard edges, your stridency and your arrogance. Your voice will acquire a quality of tenderness and your hands a quality of caring. Inwardly your being will become pure, as you follow the true longing of your spirit to love and remember the Divine.

If you persevere in your remembrance, you will no longer have so many moments of boredom, dissatisfaction or idleness. Some people become quieter as their lives take on the quality of a daily prayer. You may find yourself out of step with the hectic rhythm of the modern world, but do not lose the rhythm of your breath in order to fit in. As your remembrance becomes part of your life, and part of your breath, the pull of the material world will no longer hold you so tightly. The attraction of the Divine will hold you in Its remembrance, as you become a true lover.

RECOGNISING YOUR TRUE FACE

Through remembrance you will come to recognise your Christ like face. Your Christ like face is your true face. All human beings have this counterpart within them; it is the face of their human perfection. As your inner being becomes calm and pure, so upon the still surface of your soul the image of your true face appears, the face of Christ. In your true face, you see the Divine. Understanding your intrinsic divinity, the divinity of your essence, your soul becomes peaceful, calm and pure.

THE FLIGHT OF THE SPIRIT

As your lower soul becomes still, the flight of your spirit becomes possible. Through remembrance you have touched another reality, one that sets you free. As you see your true face, your spirit is attracted home. You experience the longing of your spirit to return, a longing that you first encountered on the stair of hope. Now you are lighter and purer and can experience this liberty of spirit without danger of inflating the ego or darkening the heart.

The experience of spiritual liberty is a feeling of freedom from all attachment to this realm, as your spirit is attracted home to the arms of the Divine. Paradoxically, however, attention to love within this earthly realm is the only way to ensure that this spiritual freedom leads to further transformation. Remembrance, and the spiritual liberty it brings, cannot alone provide you with all you need for further growth. If they are all you have, your remembrance will become sterile, and your flight will lack direction.

THE JEWEL OF SERVICE

For this reason, the next step on the stair is the one that brings you down to earth. Taking the step of remembrance you find a ruby, as you recognise your true face shining in the mirror of your soul. This recognition makes possible the ecstatic flight of your spirit. You return from the experience of spiritual freedom to take the next step on your path. Looking ahead, you see a bright blue light falling on the stair, from the sapphire window above. On the next step you will discover another jewel, one that's hidden in the earth, the jewel of service.

THE SAPPHIRE WINDOW OF SERVICE

THE HIDDEN JEWEL OF SERVICE

Service is a hidden jewel. If you don't find it, you cannot progress safely on your path, no matter how sincere your remembrance. For this reason, service is a step on any true spiritual path. Service expands your world so that the progress you have already made is shared with others, who benefit from your spiritual development. Without the step of service your progress will always be self-centred.

If you have a strong spiritual vocation, it may be hard for you to be truly committed to other relationships, because intimacy with the Divine may be the central relationship in your life. But whether your path involves a partnership with another or not, it is important that it includes some element of relationship with others. Even a hermit's path usually includes being available sometimes to counsel those in need. If you devote yourself entirely to remembrance and cut yourself off from other human contact, you may lose sight of why you are here on earth. Service brings you close to the Divine through the medium of relationships with other human beings, and with other forms of life.

RECOGNISING THE BEAUTY OF THE DIVINE IN OTHERS

You can make an attitude of service part of your life, if you so choose. In my own life I learned about service in many different ways. In caring for my children I learned to care about someone other than myself. In my work with others, I tried to see the face of Christ in the faces of those with whom I worked. I saw him in the face of a woman with an ulcerated breast, who was suffering from terminal cancer. I saw him in the eyes of a young schizophrenic homeless woman, as in between her jumbled phrases she dared to connect with me through a glance, a glance of recognition. I saw him in the stillness of a woman with Downs Syndrome, who chose to remain mute for her whole life, because of the sufferings of her institutionalised childhood. In my job as a social worker, I found the face of Christ hidden in the faces of those with whom I shared time. As I shared moments with these individuals

I recognised the privilege of knowing them, of seeing their true beauty, a beauty hidden behind the trappings of their lives.

The point I am making by sharing my experience is that you cannot follow a spiritual path all by yourself, in a kind of contemplative cocoon. You have to recognise the beauty of the spirit in everyone else, particularly in those whom others reject. It is easy to see the Divine in all that beautiful and full of grace. It is harder to see it in people whose bodies and minds may be twisted from long years of suffering. Until you recognise and revere this beauty in others, you cannot really recognise it in yourself. This is the point of service, and why it adorns every true spiritual path.

CHOOSING TO FEEL

The jewel of service is found as you deeply feel the suffering of another being. As their beauty touches you, so does their pain, because you know yourself deeply by now, and you can feel your own pain. The reason we are insensitive to the pain of others is because we are insensitive to our own, we have chosen not to feel it, to deaden it. To undertake a journey of self-knowledge and self-recovery is to accept a new way of being. This is a way that does not run away from, or try to cover up, all that you have suffered. Becoming human means becoming vulnerable, for you no longer seek to protect yourself by choosing not to feel. As you become more human you feel more, both for yourself and others.

Through your increased emotional depth, you are able to hold the pain of others, you do not brush it aside anymore. In holding it for them, you hold your own pain also, and you help to heal them both, through a look of recognition. This is a look of understanding and connection, a silent offering of hope. The greatest pain is often unconscious; it is the pain of being lost, of having forgotten our way home. There is nothing worse than feeling lost and entirely alone. Just to know that another being recognises your suffering and does not run away from it, immediately reduces the weight of your loneliness.

THE SERVICE OF TRUE RECOGNITION

If through your purity of heart you can care for another and be with them in their loneliness and suffering, seeing the divine in them and loving it, you have truly served them. The service of true recognition is the service of those who find the truth in everybody else, as well as in themselves. As you recognise the divinity of another, as your tears fall, so is the sapphire revealed. As you find a jewel in the heart of another, so this window opens in your own, revealing a stone of compassionate grace.

MAKING THE PRINCIPLE OF SERVICE PART OF YOUR LIFE
You can realise service in every occupation; it does not have to be one of the 'helping' ones. Making the principle of service part of your daily life means changing your attitude to people. First you must learn to trust them, as recognition only works through love, never through fear. Then you learn to honour them as unique individuals, and then you learn to revere them as a reflection of the Divine. To revere others is to see the beauty hidden in their heart and spirit, for we all originate in Divinity. You not only see the beauty, you also understand how the circumstances of this realm have twisted and hurt the covering on this original spark. Now the person may no longer see themselves as they are, a spark of the Divine Light.

You can feel the suffering of this twisted state, because you have been through it, you have experienced it yourself. In this way you become a truly compassionate presence, someone who can suffer with and understand the struggle that we all have, to know ourselves as we truly are. Service does not put you above anyone. It brings you together, as you recognise the truth. You see through the layers of pain that the past has wrought, to the inner reality that is always divine.

WITHOUT SERVICE NO PATH IS INCLUSIVE
Without service no path is inclusive, no path really includes anyone but you. As such, you become stuck on it eventually, finding you can go no further. To progress any further you have to take other people with you, and one way of doing this is through sincere and loving service.

DANGERS AT THIS STAGE OF THE PATH
Having discovered the treasure of remembrance and the hidden

jewel of service, your soul becomes calm and pure. It has been purified by the remembrance of your breath, and illumined by the recognition of the Divine all around you. This can be a dangerous stage; because you have climbed high, it is easy to presume that you are further along than you really are. Even though you have become trustworthy in human terms, you are not immune from spiritual pride, the pride that hides behind an angelic face. If you become proud of your own spiritual beauty, and feel that you are more illumined and compassionate than other people, you will fall. The grace of your remembrance will only hold you up as long as you remain humble. When you start to think you are better than others, you will become deluded and disconnected, and start to lose your way.

THE DANGER THAT LIES BEHIND AN ILLUMINED STATE OF BEING

Everyone who goes this far on a spiritual path, at some time or other meets their spiritual pride. This is because it is impossible to climb high without it rising within you. If you have been well taught, if you have learned the lessons of the stairs below, you will recognise the angelic face of your pride, and see through it. You will see through the illusion of your ego, which always wants to play at being God. You will understand the danger that lies behind an illumined state of being. You will see through the flattery of others, and recognise when it begins to inflate your inner being and swell your head. You will seek insight into your own areas of weakness. You will be happy to serve, for in service you will find safety, and a sense of purpose.

THE NEED FOR BALANCE

As you progress on a path the higher you climb, the more you need balance. It is important to balance inner and outer worlds, activity and contemplation, remembrance and service. If you follow an unbalanced path, you may veer too near the edge. You will be more susceptible to your own delusions and pretensions, and those of others; it will be easier to lose your footing and fall.

Because of your wisdom and experience by now, you may recognise this danger, the danger of the highest stair. You will understand that you are not yet ready to guide, because even though you have experienced spiritual ascent, you are still constrained by the limits of your identity. For this reason the next step on the path is unity, the step where you make a horizontal shift in perception, and dissolve in the light.

LEAVING BEHIND A VERTICAL PERSPECTIVE

With the step of unity you will cease to be on a vertical path, and ideas of higher or lower will no longer apply. This is why you must take this step before you can guide others with safety. If you do not your perception of the path may be of a ladder of ascent, where you stand at the top. This is an erroneous view. To guide home, you need to have a different perspective, a complete and rounded understanding of the nature of spiritual growth, and it's true purpose.

The true goal of your path is not at the top of a ladder, although this may be how you saw it in your youth, because this may be how you viewed achievement then. Now, in spiritual adulthood, it is time to leave behind a vertical perspective and embrace a new way of seeing. If you do not, you will remain at a stage where many people become stranded. This is a stage of individual spiritual illumination, where you think yourself more illumined than others because you stand above them. You cannot go any further as you are limited by this way of seeing; if you remain at the top of a ladder, there is nowhere else you can go. To progress you have to leave the ladder behind, and step towards unity. This step will bring you a new perspective, a new direction, and a new humility.

You cannot reach the step of unity through the application of your will, no matter how hard you try. It is reached through surrender. You surrender your individual path as you leave behind the ladder of attainment on which you climbed so high. Turning towards the next step, you feel warm green rays descending on you from the emerald window above, the window of unity.

THE EMERALD WINDOW OF UNITY

THE JEWEL OF UNITY

The light of unity helps you to progress from a self-oriented viewpoint to a more universal understanding. Through the step of unity, you leave behind all sense of limitation, and experience the truth of the unity of being. Unity is a jewel of transformation, just as patience is. The jewel of unity transforms your perception of your world, your path, and your destination.

A DEFINITION OF UNITY

An intellectual definition of unity is that there is nothing but God, or the Goddess, or the One Universal Being, or the Great Spirit – whatever your particular name for the Divine is. To grasp this truth, is to understand that from childhood we have been taught to perceive duality. We have seen our world in terms of I and you, us and them, here and there, up and down, near and far etc. We have learned to see the world in a way that splits it up, and that separates us from it. This way of seeing helped us to develop as children and adults with a healthy sense of self. However, at this stage of the path we can look again at this framework of learning and realise that it does not correspond to reality. We can only know this for sure by direct perception, not by being told. An intellectual understanding of unity cannot transform spiritual consciousness; for this an experiential understanding is needed.

Direct perception of unity is the experience of the unity of being. In this experience you lose yourself, and understand that there is only One Universal Being, and this Being is without boundaries. As you let go of yourself, your sense of separation from everything else dissolves, and there is no 'you', there is only One.

YOUR MOTIVATION FOR TAKING THIS STEP

If you are ready for this step, you will have reached a certain level of understanding. You will be ready to lose your limitations in unity's light. Your motivation for wanting to take this step will determine how you reach it, and if you progress beyond it. The sincerity of your aspiration is important. If you want to experience unity to achieve a spiritual high that makes your life more interesting, you may not benefit from the experience. If you want to experience unity in order to heal your vision and help you see the truth, your sincerity will bring you to this step, and maybe beyond it. If you want to reach the stage of unity to succeed on your path, if your motives are purely ambitious, you may reach this step but you will not understand its deeply compassionate dimension.

In the chapter on trust I talked of the connection to all life that enables us to become fully human. Unity is really an extension of this connection, which also expands the boundaries of our love and trust. At the stage of trust we are still present, as we connect to all life. At the stage of unity we lose our sense of separation, we lose our self-consciousness, and cease to see ourselves as separate from anything.

THE STEP OF UNITY FROM A MODERN PERSPECTIVE

To experience unity, first you have to let go of the idea of being separate. To let go of the idea of being you is to allow yourself to feel your connection to the whole of creation, in an energetic way. We think we live in separate bodies, but in truth we are energy. Our thoughts define the limitations of our world, but in truth we are not limited. Opening up to the experience of unity is opening up your consciousness to the sea of universal energy all around you. You understand that the truth is we are the sea, waves within it that are identical in essence to the rest of the ocean. You no longer think you are swimming in this ocean, you allow yourself to drown in it, to discover the truth of your being. This truth is that all life is One.

Experiencing unity means losing the barriers that you thought separated you from the world around you. You are the sadness of a friend, you are the beauty of a sunset, you are the power of a storm. This is both a liberating and an uncomfortable way to feel. It is liberating because you are freed from any limitation; you become all of creation. It is sometimes uncomfortable because it is difficult to feel the pain and fear of others, without any protective barriers, the barriers of your normal selfhood. You may feel defenceless in this state, without a defined edge to your world. You will become very sensitive to disharmonious atmospheres, and disharmonious people. At the same time you will feel exhilarated because of the boundlessness of your consciousness.

CONNECTING TO THE SOUL OF ALL LIFE

As you come back to yourself from the experience of unity, everything is different. Although you assume your selfhood again, at a deeper level of your being you recognise your connection to the soul of all life. You no longer live in isolation. You are the growing planet; you are the ever-evolving human family.

Feeling this deep soul connection with all life you experience humility, joy, compassion and peace. Humility, for you realise how small was your perception before, and how alone you felt. You understand that we are all interdependent, and that while you are not that important on your own, as part of something bigger all of us are precious. Joy, because you have experienced the well spring of all life, a spring that never runs dry, that you can recover through a sense of deep inner connection. Compassion, because you truly participate in the suffering of all life in its struggle to evolve, and through your level of understanding help to heal it. Peace, because there is nothing left to strive for, nothing left to fight for. Having experienced unity, you have tasted truth.

A CHANGE IN PERSPECTIVE

One result of this experience is that you cease to see the spiritual path in a vertical way. You now see it from a circular perspective, for this is the perspective of unity. You are no longer at the top, you are no longer there as a separate being. Only love is there, encompassing all without limit, in an expanding circle of joy. In the centre of the circle is a point of light, radiating outwards. This is the same point of light that you find in your heart through the door of faith. The truth that outlives all worlds lies within you, for this is where you find the truth of unity's point, a point of universal love.

THE STEP OF UNITY THROUGH THE AGES

This is a description of what it feels like to experience the unity of being, using modern language to explain an age-old process. Sincere aspirants have been taking this step through the ages, using the framework of the spiritual traditions of their time. At this stage in humanity's growth, you do not have to belong to any particular spiritual tradition to take the step of unity. The experience of unity is really the experience of universal love; this is the point to which unity will lead you, whichever path you take to reach it.

The spiritual traditions of the past kept alight a path to grace for us through the centuries, and we should respect and value all that they still have to teach us. I will now give a brief and limited description of the experience of unity, as it occurs within two established spiritual traditions. I hope that this may be of interest to some, and of relevance to any on a Sufi or a Christian path.

UNITY FROM THE PERSPECTIVE OF ISLAMIC SUFISM
The affirmation of Divine Unity: 'La illaha ill'Allah' is the cornerstone of the Islamic faith. Translated this means: 'There is no God, but God.' In other words there is nothing, except God (who is everything). Duality is rejected, for the truth is One, and this One is Allah. To make this affirmation inwardly, rather than just reciting it outwardly, you must tread the inner path of Islam. This is the path of the Sufi.

THE EXPERIENCE OF THE UNITY OF BEING
To affirm the inner truth of Divine Unity, you need to experience the unity of being. When you lose self-consciousness, you experience nothingness. In this state you lose the perspective of your limited ego. Losing the perspective of the self you open your consciousness to the experience of the truth, which is the experience of 'but God'.

You now understand that you are not a separate being, that you are part of the One Being that always was, always will be, that was never born and can never die. To say that you are part is not really accurate, we are all part and yet we are all total also. We are the consciousness of the many in the One, and the consciousness of the One in the many. Your consciousness spans a circle, the circle of unity, a spiritual ring from which all manifest form descends. The circle of unity contracts to a point in your consciousness, this point being both the origin, and the end, of all created dimensions.

THE EXPERIENCE OF TIMELESSNESS AND PLACELESSNESS
In this point you always were, and therefore now your conscious-ness spans all time. In this point you always are, and therefore now

your consciousness spans all space. And yet there is no end to time and space. The linear and dimensional models of time and space that you erected from your limited perspective no longer exist. Time always was beginning and ending, and in spirals revolves around a central point. Space always is contracting and expanding and in circles moves away from and towards a central point. This central point is the point of Unity, the point from which all created dimensions spring, and to which they will all return. In this way the experience of timelessness and placelessness is realised. You are lost in the experience of awe as you participate in the eternal grandeur and beauty of the One Point that you have always loved (that has always loved Itself).

THE AFFIRMATION OF UNITY

'No God, but God', is the central affirmation of Unity in the Islamic Sufi tradition. From here one can progress to 'no You, but You' and finally to the truest expression of unity one can affirm which is: 'no I, but I'. In this experience of selflessness one loses the claim to have an individual I. You lose your I, and you truly experience the One through Itself, without any intermediary. This is the highest affirmation of unity you can make, and the most misunderstood.

Those who make such a profession with sincerity are no longer conscious of themselves, and so what comes out of their mouths is pure truth. They are no longer there to experience unity in terms of a being outside of what was once them. It cannot be called God or He, She or You. In all honesty all they can say is 'there is no I, but I'. They are no longer there; the Truth is there. As such they speak in trance, and are entirely inspired.

THE AFFIRMATION OF HALLAJ

One who realised such a profession of unity was Mansur-al-Hallaj. In his ecstatic state he proclaimed 'I am the Truth'. The clerics of his time did not understand him, called him a heretic for claiming to be God, imprisoned him and eventually crucified him. He had realised the reality of unity to such a degree that even his cruel death did not destroy his ecstatic state. He danced to the cross in a trance of love. I mention him here because his affirmation of unity is the most sublime.

UNITY FROM A CHRISTIAN PERSPECTIVE

In the Christian tradition the experience of unity is connected to an understanding of the teaching of the Body of Christ. The Christ light shone through the form of Jesus, but its existence is not limited to one human body. This light can shine through each one of us, as we recognise our true identity. The experience of recognising at onement with the universal spirit of the Christ is the main purpose behind the sacrament of communion. Through ritually sharing in the body and blood of one who gave his body for the many, the many experience the oneness of the Christ. When we connect with this light we connect with all of those who were part of this Universal Body before us, and who will be after. We discover the true meaning of communion through the experience of losing our limited self, and becoming part of One Body that always was and is. It is a sublime doctrine that when understood experientially always leads to unity and grace.

UNIVERSAL COMMUNION

Through true communion you lose your limited consciousness to be contained within the Body of the Christ. The communion in Christ is the first step to universal communion. Universal communion is when the Body of Christ dissolves in the universal love that is its essence. This dissolution is our spiritual liberation from all boundaries of time, place, and matter. This is the dissolution that precedes the resurrection. The resurrection is the consciousness of universal love and grace that is no longer contained. The All now has no boundaries, no body; it is universal love that always was and always will be. Through our communion with the Body of Christ we are led to experience universal love.

THE TRINITY FROM THE PERSPECTIVE OF UNITY

It can be helpful to see the trinity as three steps on a ladder that leads you to understand the Oneness of God. The first step is the Holy Spirit, the bird that inspires and leads you to the grace of the Christ. The second step is the Son, the Body of the Christ that you join with in order to lose your separation, and which brings you the grace of communion. The last step is the Father, the universal loving consciousness that always was and will be.

This you are led to through the communion in Christ. As the Universal Body of the Christ dissolves you are liberated into an understanding of the boundlessness of love that is an everlasting resurrection.

THE POINT OF UNIVERSAL LOVE

In these three steps you attain to unity, to the resurrection of universal love. Within universal love (the Father) all is, including the Son and the Holy Spirit. The One holds all and yet cannot be held; it has no boundaries to be contained by. Within its boundlessness there is a central point, the point you celebrate in the sacrament of communion. For the love of the many one gave himself, that the many might understand the point of universal love. The message of the cross, the message of the resurrection, and the message of Holy Communion are the same. They lead to the same point, the point which is at the heart of all spiritual evolution, all the Son's teaching, all the Spirit's inspiration, and all the Father's creation. In the end, all true spiritual paths lead to the same point, a point of universal love.

LOSING A LIMITED PERSPECTIVE

There are many ways to unity. All that is required is a willingness to leave behind limited methods of experiencing and perceiving, and a sincerity of intent. To experience unity on any of its levels means that you lose the limited perception of yourself, the universe, and the nature of reality that you had before. As such it is a big step on your evolutionary journey. Until you understand experientially that you have no boundaries, and that all life is an expression of the energy of love, you have an erroneous view of everything. After the experience of the unity of being, you lose your pride, as you understand that all of us are equal, because essentially we are all the same. We are all love, and we are all loved.

The three paths to the experience of unity that I have described, are not the only ways to reach it. There are other tried and trusted paths, such as the path of the Buddha. All the great world religions and their teachers will lead you to this step, if you follow their inner teaching with sincere aspiration.

OTHER AVENUES TO UNITY

If you would like to experience unity, and are getting nowhere, do not worry. This may mean that you are not yet ready for this experience. It cannot be achieved by an effort of will, no matter how hard you try. Try instead to bring the energy of loving compassion into your life. If you are faithful in service eventually you may see your Beloved in the ones you serve. This too is an avenue to unity, the avenue of the purest.

If you have a teacher, they may become a doorway through which you pass, to lose yourself in the light of the Truth. A teacher can be such a doorway, and so can other relationships. If you truly love someone, they can be a doorway through which you lose your self-identity, to find the Divine in them, and in yourself. An intimate love relationship can be an avenue to unity, as long as the other person becomes for you a window to the Truth, rather than an idol that you worship for its own sake.

SHORTCUTS TO UNITY

Some people have tried by using narcotics like LSD to experience this state, to lose the boundaries of self and experience oneness. Although you can experience unity this way, it may not help your progress in the long term. Becoming a trustworthy human being is the first step towards spiritual maturity on any true path. If you take the step of unity too soon, it may confuse you, and hinder your future growth.

When the unified state of consciousness wears off you may have to struggle with your own conceit, as you may think that you have understood everything, and that there is nothing left for you to learn. You cannot share the jewel of unity until you have learned to hold a human trust. Until you are a trustworthy human being you will not be able to share it, no matter how much you know, and no matter how much you have experienced.

SELF-ABANDONMENT ON A PATH TO CHAOS

There are some paths that appear to lead to an experience of unity, that should be approached with caution. There is a way sometimes chosen by self-interested teachers, that involves an experience of loss of self-consciousness. On this way the experience of unity involves a breaking down of the sense of self, through the breaking down of an individual's personal and social frames of reference.

The experience of challenging and breaking taboos is seen as a way of reaching a state of increased awareness. In the experience of freedom from social constraint, the individual experiences a loss of selfhood as they are swept along by the energy of abandonment. This energy has a strong momentum, and a strong attraction. It is released in group settings where social and personal inhibitions are broken down, sometimes through the practice of group sex. In such practices some find a sense of freedom, freedom from illusions about themselves and their world. In the energy of abandonment they may find a point of stillness, which they may mistake for the point of truth.

THE ENERGY OF CHAOS

The point of stillness they have found on such a path is a point of involuntary return. It is like a moment of stillness on the edge of a black hole, just before everything is sucked in. It is not the point of unity from which creation originates, it cannot expand outwards to create anything new. The energy of chaos takes you down, and tears apart, it cannot bring together. This is because the energy of chaos in which you can lose yourself contains no compassion. It has no healing energy to mend and make well. It is the energy of involution, it can only take you down, it cannot help you to evolve.

CIRCLES WITHOUT TRUST

Behind such a path you will always find a self-interested teacher who is neither brave nor strong. They will seek to manipulate and control the energy of the group, because they have not yet understood for themselves the point of unity that heals the circle. Their teaching groups will be rings that shed no light; circles without trust that share no lasting truth. Such a teacher has not found any true liberation or peace within themselves. True liberation is the liberation of universal love, that turns all illusion aside, and celebrates an everlasting point of truth, not one that is temporary.

A HARMONIOUS RETURN TO LOVE

To evolve gracefully you need to find an everlasting point of truth in your own being. To find this point you have to learn how to love. This awakens your spiritual consciousness, the part of you that longs to return to your origin. Then your return will be voluntary and harmonious, a conscious return to the true point within you, a point of universal love. The energy of compassion is the energy that takes you home to an everlasting point. It is the energy that leads to grace. This is the energy behind all true paths that lead to unity, and from here to grace.

KNOWING WHICH PATH YOU ARE ON

Just as unity is a major step on a path to grace, so the anarchy of self-abandonment is a major step on a path to chaos. Do not confuse the two; the only similarity they have is that both include a temporary loss of self-consciousness. This loss leads to understanding if you are on a true path, but to confusion if you are on a path of self-interest. You will always know which path you are on, by the way you feel.

The step of unity will leave you feeling humble and peaceful. You will stand in your own light as you find within you the strength of your true point. The step of self-abandonment will at first leave you feeling elated, energised and with a heightened sense of awareness. But, just like a narcotic, when the euphoria wears off you will feel empty and cold, and you will need some more. Once on such a path you will become increasingly dependent. You will need another draught from the cup of chaos to dispel fresh waves of despair.

A PATH TO PEACE

Sometimes such paths are presented as taking people back to a connection with the earth, with nature and with the natural world. To connect with nature is deeply healing, and nature is compassionate, offering us healing grace with many plants and herbs. A path that truly embraces nature will bring you to trust, to patience and to compassionate peace. The way of the native Americans who understood the balance and harmony of the natural world is such a path. A path to chaos is not a true path of nature, for it has no creative point. It will not lead you to find a peaceful point within yourself.

BRINGING YOUR EXPERIENCE OF UNITY DOWN TO EARTH

As you journey more deeply into unity, you will find that it takes you more deeply into relationship with others, for this is how you realise its true point. You will begin to understand unity from a human perspective. To do this you need to transform your experience of unity so that you understand it on the ground as well as in the sky. It is not enough to experience the grandeur of the universe in which you are dissolved. You also need to feel the kinship of the circle, holding in your heart all creatures who are your brothers and sisters.

Unless you bring your understanding of unity down to a level whereby it connects you in a deeply democratic way to all life, then you have not really understood the point of it. The point of unity is found in universal love, and you express this outwardly in your life through loving service. Understanding the compassionate point of unity, as you love your human and animal family more and more, you earn the emerald hidden in unity's window. This is the precious stone that has illumined your vision and changed your world.

THE CIRCLE OF UNITY

Through the step of unity, you join a circle where you share a trust of peace. In the centre of this circle is the Divine Light, the light that all around the circle embody, as there is nothing but this light in many different forms. This light emanates from a central point, the point that through your own spiritual path you have come to know and understand. This is a permanent point of calm, a point of universal unconditional love. Thus, unity reconnects you with life, and the circle of unity is one that reveres all forms of life, and brings them the light of peace.

SHARING THE CUP OF UNITY

When you have experienced this level of unity, you are ready to become a priest, or priestess, if this is your calling. Whatever spiritual tradition you belong to, you are now fit to perform the role that a true priest or priestess has always performed. You are ready to hold the cup of the spirit, as you share the blessing of peace. You are able through your inner spiritual experience to unite others through a ritual sharing of this cup.

This communion was effected through different rituals in different cultures, but the purpose was always the same. The Priest, or Elder, or Sheikh, or Shaman is one who unites the community in which he or she lives, through a ritual sharing, during which the light of his or her spiritual illumination is shared with the rest. If the priest is illumined by a particular teacher (such as Jesus) then it is the grace of this teacher that the community receives. The priest becomes a channel for their light. This light connects them to the Divine Light of the One (the Father or Mother) in whom all dissolve.

THE ROLE OF A PRIEST

The priest is one who is both a channel and a conductive body. He or she both receives grace, and transmits it to all the people who are present with him or her for the ritual. In this way the true priests of every culture hold communities together, and spread the light of truth and brother/sisterhood that keeps their community spiritually healthy.

The light that a true priest shares is the light of their true point, the light that is hidden within all manifest creation. The vessel that they share it through is their human form, which has awakened to its own divine essence, and to the united essence of creation. Their human form is the grail, the cup, for the uncreated light of their spirit. Their spiritual path has led them through self-knowledge to hold a human trust, and ultimately to hold the grail, so that they may share it with the rest. The wine within the cup of the true priest is their enlightened spiritual essence, and this brings forgiveness and the blessing of peace, as all are united through its true light.

PRIESTS OF THE SHADOW

Without true priests to hold the grail, to channel and transmit grace, communities cannot share a common healing spiritual experience. They cease to hold together, and people lose their individual way for lack of light. The priests of the shadow are those teachers who spread confusion and dependency. The wine within their cup brings intoxication without illumination. Their spiritual essence is not pure, for they are driven by selfish goals. If people have no experience of a communal sharing of the peace of grace through the energy of a true priest, then some of them may be attracted to the ceremonies of such teachers. These promise communion of a sort, but one that is ultimately barren.

THE STABILITY OF A TRUE PRIEST

A true priest has united the opposites within him or herself, and now possesses unified vision. They fear no evil for they have seen through it, and they know that nothing exists outside the reality of unity. Even the excesses of false teachers they understand to be the mirror image of the true path, for everything in existence has a reflection. But the reflection is not the truth, it is only a temporary shadow that depends on the truth for its existence. True priests have found a permanent point of light within themselves, in the point of universal love, to which all dimensions return. Therefore they fear no reflection, and see through those teachers whose paths have no true point. In the heart of a true priest is found the light that guides, a guidance that they share with others through faith, hope and kindness.

THE POWER OF UNIVERSAL LOVE

Unfortunately, many priests are not trained to understand experientially the truth of unity that gives them spiritual strength and power. There is no power greater than that of universal love, and until you stand firm in this power, you are not truly strong, and you cannot protect others from fear of evil. However, whatever the limitations in formal training, there have always been, and there will always be, a few true priests and priestesses, who are led and taught by their own inner light. They are the ones whose spiritual flame brings light and peace to their communities, and whose human qualities inspire others to be pure of heart.

THE END OF YOUR JOURNEY?

Unity is the last window in the wall of the tower, and it may be that your spiritual journey ends here. You have travelled far enough to be a true priest, a bringer of light and blessing to others; far enough to be a trustworthy human being, a peacemaker, one on whom others can depend. You have reached a stage where you can share the cup of eternal light and peace. This is an achievement in any age. To go further may require a certain sacrifice, and it may be that this will not further your calling, or your life purpose on earth.

THE WINDOW OF FRIENDSHIP

However, it may be that unity is not the last step on your path. Looking up you may realise that there is one last window, one that you never noticed before, although you have always received its light. It is a circular window in the roof above you, different from all the other windows on the steps below. They were arch shaped openings that lit the spiral stair. The window of friendship is a large round window in the roof of the tower; it is inlaid with precious stones set in a golden frame.

You see diamonds for purity, rubies for remembrance, sapphires for service, and emeralds for unity, arranged in a kaleidoscopic pattern of great beauty. You marvel at the beauty of it, for this window is slowly turning, and the jewels change their patterns as the window turns. Light is streaming down from this window, spilling multi-coloured patterns onto the stairs below. Looking down you see how all the steps in the tower receive light from the window of friendship, for it is the main window in the tower, a huge disc of turning coloured light. You have found your way to the window that brings light to all the others, the window of the treasury of friends.

CENTRAL WINDOW IN THE
ROOF OF THE TOWER

5

The Window of Friendship

THE WINDOW OF FRIENDSHIP

Under the window of friendship you realise that you have always found your way with the help of this window's light, although formerly you did not know it was there. Standing beneath the turning window you feel the friendship of all who helped you arrive at this step. Receiving their light, you understand what it is to be a true friend.

THE GIFT OF TRUE FRIENDS

Those who befriend you through this light are those who have existed at different times and places in history, they are usually no longer existent in this realm. You receive from them the gift that true friends and teachers always give, spiritual support, sound counsel, encouragement and an example to follow. You receive from them the communion of spirit that banishes the sadness of those whose spiritual quest is a lonely one. Through their friendship you are rewarded for your sincerity of purpose and your purity of intention. It has always been so. There have always been true friends in spirit who support and help the sincere aspirant who needs their help.

Through understanding the depth of their friendship, you realise that the friends have always been there for you. Without true friends in spirit, none of us would have the strength to climb the stair alone. Their light gave you the faith, hope and courage to go on, during dark times when you lost your way.

BECOMING A TRUE GUIDE

As you take the step of friendship you are ready to be a friend to others; you are ready to be a spiritual guide.

To reach this stage you will have attained wisdom and spiritual strength through self-knowledge. Because you know yourself you will be a trustworthy teacher, one who has held up a mirror to their own pride and conceit. Whatever your means of earning a living in the world, your true calling is to be a guide, a friend whose being helps others to find their way home. You will not necessarily teach in a formal way, but through the illumined energy of your heart, and the pure radiance of your soul.

You will have light to share, an unending supply of light, for you have accessed the light of unity, and of friendship, and are able to share this radiance with your brothers and sisters. You are able to help them discover this light within themselves, by helping them open a door in their hearts, the door of faith.

NOWHERE LEFT TO GO BUT LOVE

There have never been many true guides, and there never will be. This is because most aspirants lose patience and start to teach others before they are ready. You are only ready to guide when you have nowhere left to go but love. Then you no longer identify with the particular, you identify with the whole, and you exist to help your brothers, for they are all part of you. You can only guide people to where you are. If you have found the point of universal love within yourself, you will lead them here. A true guide is one who guides others to love, with love, for love.

A RESPONSIBILITY TO GUIDE

At the step of friendship your path may end. You have understood the purpose of your path, and are able to lead others as a true guide. If you have come this far on your path, you have a responsibility to share with others the way that you have found, to help others return. In this way a human path is kept open through the ages, through the dedication of true guides, who keep the path alight for future generations.

THE INVITATION OF THE FRIENDS

For a few people however, this step is not the end of their path. If you are one of them, as you stand on the step of friendship the round window above you will open. Through the open window you will see a fire, and around the fire a circle of figures in a ring of flame. These are the spirits of those who befriended you and guided you through the years. They are the pure souls who were a support and encouragement to you on your path, who stood by you, who sent you light, who helped you find your way. You now realise that this window has opened as an invitation, and that you are being invited to join this circle round the fire.

A DIFFERENT PATH

If you pass through the window you will tread a different path. Few people will share your experience, or know where you are. You will be a pioneer, and you will share the loneliness of all true pioneers. And yet you will have peers. Your peers will span the ages, for they will be all of those who passed beyond unity before, to friendship, and from here to grace. They will now be your companions on the path, and it is they who wait for you on the other side of the window. Recognising your spirit as one that may want to go on, they gently call you to rise and come forward.

A FREE CHOICE

If you so choose, you will pass through the open window into the fire, to join the friends. If you choose not to go, the window above you will close. In true spiritual development there is never any pressure; you always have free will. There is always a choice, and whichever path you choose will bring you something that will help you learn.

If you are not yet ready for the depth of experience promised in the fire, you will stay where you are. You will stay at the step of friendship, and as you do so a handful of jewels will rain down on you from the window above, as it gently closes. The diamonds, rubies, sapphires and emeralds you receive are a token of your progress so far, the treasury found in the pure heart of a friend. Through such a heart others will receive the blessing that the friends have shared with you. The window of friendship will continue to illumine you for the rest of your life. You will be able to share this light with all who come to you for assistance, and to all of them you will be a true friend.

CHOOSING THE FIRE

If you choose to go through the window and into the fire, you will understand what this choice involves. To join the ring of friends is to join a spiritual order that has existed from the beginning. This order is one that exists to uphold the spiritual health of humanity, and it has always been present, through the dark ages, through the modern ages, throughout time. Because you have been liberated from your own limited conception of time and space, through the experience of unity and its point, you may be invited to join the friends. You are only invited to do so, if you have proved your sincerity of intent, your compassion, and your lack of self-interest. The purpose of this order is service to humanity.

The friends in the fire choose to stay here in order to bring the light of spiritual illumination, assistance and understanding to all of their brothers and sisters below, who are struggling to see and understand. They choose to do this from motives of unconditional love, for this is the point that they reached in their own spiritual journey, when incarnate in form. The fire in the centre burns through the energy they bring to it. They choose to stay and feed the fire, a fire that is fed by the light of their love and knowledge. This fire also reflects the light from another fire high above in the centre of the rooftop domes, the fire of grace.

THE ORDER OF THE FRIENDS
The friends choose to stay here in the fire, rather than to ascend to lighter levels of being, which would leave the concerns of the earth behind. They no longer need to incarnate on earth, and they are evolved enough to continue their existence in other worlds and realms of light, but they choose not to do so. They choose to stay close to humanity, to keep the fire going, and to thereby bring their brother's light.

They choose to do this because they do not want to leave their brothers and sisters behind in the dark. Because once they struggled in this realm, they know that they could not have ascended this far without the light of friends who kept alive a fire for them. Thus, they choose to stay here through the ages and keep this fire alive, for all of those still to come. One name for this circle is the Order of the Friends. This is the spiritual rank given to those who consciously and selflessly choose to stay behind, for the sake of their younger brothers and sisters who need light.

A PERSONAL CHOICE
You realise as you make your choice, that this choice is one you always wanted to make. Because you have nowhere left to go but love, you realise that this fire is your path's true destination. You realise that choosing not to go through the window, but to remain in freedom

where you are, is not what you want to do. You understand that you do not want to progress from incarnations on earth, up to lighter realms of spirit, that this is not where you want to go.

This is because you see that all spiritual ascent, all future lifetimes that you might experience in worlds of light, will ultimately lead you to the same point of understanding that you will find in the fire. You realise that if you choose the freedom of a lighter state of being, you may pass through many ascending levels of evolutionary consciousness, and many further initiations, to eventually reach the same point of understanding that you will find in the fire. This is the understanding of pure universal love. Whether you realise it in the fire, or in the highest realm as you take the final initiation, this point will be the same.

AN EVOLUTIONARY LEAP

As you realise this, there is nowhere else for you to go but the fire. For the point of pure universal love that you find in the fire, will be the same one that you arrive at eventually, whatever choice you make. Through being offered the fire, you are being offered an evolutionary leap that will save you much time. Through the breadth of your illumined understanding, and the depth of your compassion, you are able to make this choice, and pass through the window into the fire. You leap with open arms into the fire, where the others welcome you as a new friend.

THE RING OF FRIENDS

Having passed through the window, you take your place in the centre of the fire. Every new arrival knows that their place is in the centre, until the next aspirant arrives. As you begin to burn you understand that the circle of friends is the foundation of this world's spiritual order. Without the light of the ring of friends, humankind would not have enough spiritual energy to help them progress and evolve. Creation would have descended into chaos long ago, for the delicate balance between light and dark, spirit and matter, would not have held together.

The ring of true friends upholds the balance of both the created and the spiritual worlds. This means that this ring's light is essential for the existing balance of the world of spirit, and the world of matter. Without friends, the light of truth would find no reflection on the spiritual path, or in the created world. Without such a mirror, spiritual form and physical manifestation would disintegrate and return in chaos to non-existence. Thus, the ring of friends both keeps the path alight, and preserves the order and balance of the spiritual and material worlds.

THE LIGHT OF OUR HUMANITY

This is why there have been individuals in every time, who were destined to join the friends in the fire, thereby renewing its light and upholding the balance of the two worlds. To do so they must have reached a state of being whereby they understood the point of universal love, otherwise they would not be conscious enough to make this choice.

Thus there have always been friends and teachers, incarnate or in spirit, to teach Adam's children how to become conscious enough to make this choice. The first friend and teacher was Adam's own divine light, the light of his humanity. His fall was his forgetfulness of this light, the light of pure universal love. All of us possess Adam's light in the heart, but we sometimes need help remembering it. It is this light that all true friends and teachers radiate, so that we can become conscious of it in ourselves. It is consciousness of this light, and its point within, that enables you to choose to burn for everyone else.

THE ILLUMINATION OF THIS RING

All the earliest teachers of humanity had reached this level in their spiritual evolution, and thus brought to mankind the illumination of this ring. From their light, humankind learned how to be tolerant, unselfish, honest, just and kind. Through the influence of this light on the hearts and minds of men, humanity was helped to evolve to a higher level of being. Through the ages all true brotherhoods reflected this ring's light in their own circles, and attempted to spread its warmth and illumination. On your path until now, you have felt the warmth of this fire, and the promise of its light. You have felt it through the guidance of true teachers, or through the spiritual support of pure souls who helped you on your way. The support of the circle of trust that you felt at an earlier stage of the path, was a reflection of this ring's essence on a lower level of manifestation.

THE KINSHIP OF THE FIRE

The individual who has entered the fire of friendship shows no outward sign of their inner choice. This step needs no outer recognition or confirmation. Their confirmation inwardly comes from a sense of kinship with the spirits in the fire, to whom they are now inwardly connected. They can communicate through the telepathy of the heart with the friends in the fire, whenever they need help or guidance.

The existence of this circle of friends is a spiritual reality. Although I have described it in visionary terms, it is not a 'vision' or a 'fantasy'. It is a ring that indicates a certain level of being. To reach this level involves a choice, a choice that you can only make if you have reached a certain level of understanding. If you have not reached this level of understanding yet, you will not choose the fire. You will only choose it if you understand what it's for, if you have discovered its point within yourself.

RENEWING THE LIGHT OF THE WINDOWS IN THE TOWER

As the newcomer sits in the fire, the round window beneath them closes, and they know that there is no going back. As the spirit of the newcomer burns, the light of the fire is renewed. As the fire burns, the ring of flames around it begins to burn brightly, increasing in illumination and warmth. Light from the fire and its ring streams down through the window of friendship. The new spirit in the centre of the fire knows that they have brought light to their brothers and sisters below. They remember what it was like to climb the stair alone, to be confused, to be uncertain, to be in need of light. Around the fire the friends are smiling through the flames, as they watch the centre point of the fire beginning to rise, carrying with it the spirit of a new friend.

THE PILLAR OF FLAME

As the fire burns the newcomer looks up, and sees a window above them, identical to the one beneath them that has closed. They realise that the window of friendship has two panes, one facing downwards, the other facing upwards, and that the fire burns in between them. As the fire begins to burn more fiercely, the upper window opens. As the window above them opens, the new friend is lifted unexpectedly upwards, carried by a pillar of flame rising from the centre of the fire they have renewed. They rise in wonder, in a fountain of flame, up through the open window into the domes of grace.

ENTERING THE DOMES OF GRACE

They rise as a spirit into the domes, realising with surprise that the fire is the point of access to another realm, and that there is no other way to enter. It is not possible to enter the domes of grace by wanting to get there. You can only enter them when you have chosen for love to burn for everyone else. If your motive for bringing light to the others is to enter the domes, you will not be invited into the fire. You are only invited when you have nowhere left to go but love. Then your ascent will take you by surprise, as you thought the fire was the end of your journey, as your love is the point of the fire. In this way your spiritual transformation is made complete, and your spirit ascends into the domes of grace, while you are still living as a human being on earth. Within the domes you continue your spiritual journey.

A NEW STAGE OF THE JOURNEY

Thus you discover that the step of friendship is not the end of your path, but the beginning of a new stage. Passing through the lower and upper windows of friendship, you have reached another level, the rooftop domes of grace. Here there are no steps, your spirit will fly from dome to dome. In each dome coloured rings of light are turning. Each of the domes has windows that reflect rays of light from the rings of grace down to humanity below. In the domes you will journey through the rings of grace and understand their attributes and symbols. This last stage of the homeward journey will increase your knowledge, your understanding, your compassion and your grace, so that you have more to share.

WINDOWS IN THE DOMES OF GRACE

6

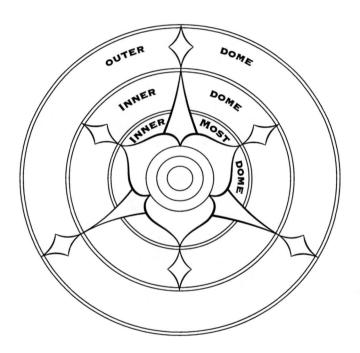

Windows in the Outer Dome
◆
Windows in the Inner Dome
◆
Windows in the Innermost Dome

WINDOWS IN THE DOMES OF GRACE

The return to grace where the spirit is illumined by the lights of grace

The last stage of the journey is one of effortless ascension, as the spirit rises upwards and inwards through the domes of grace. The three domes are arranged one above the other, becoming gradually smaller as they ascend. In the middle of the innermost, uppermost dome is the window of grace, a round window that can be seen from the centre of the lower domes.

Rings of coloured light are turning around in the domes. These originate from a point at the top of the innermost dome, the point of creative unity. This point expands outwards and downwards, to form concentric circles of coloured light. These are the rings of grace, the spiritual essence of the domes. These rings manifest different aspects of the energy of grace, different sounds, colours and vibrations.

As the spirit rises on its journey, it experiences the energy of the rings, as it assimilates the light of each one. Through the light of the rings the spirit is illumined and nourished, and comes to understand the inner attributes of grace. Every ring in the domes has a window through which its light descends to illumine the levels below. It radiates through the spiritual realm down to the densest level of matter. An angel is associated with each ray, reflecting a particular aspect of grace, the aspect that colours the original ring.

In the forthcoming chapters there is a section that describes the nature of each ray of grace, and its effect on those who receive it. There is also a section explaining in detail how you can ask for and receive the rays, so that they may illumine your own being.

The domes of grace are a step on the evolutionary ladder, a step you take after you realise your purpose on earth, both individually and collectively. This stage involves expanding your consciousness to embrace a spiritual realm, the realm of the domes of grace. This is a realm that exists outside of you, for the spiritual realm underpins the manifest universe. It also exists within you, for every human being contains a copy of the universe in miniature within their form. You become conscious of this inner realm through your increasing depth of being.

Embarking on this stage of the journey means that you grow in spiritual and emotional depth, and that, if anything, you become more fully human than you were before. This is because in the domes you are taught the deeper aspects of those qualities that ennoble the human race. In this way you understand how we are all made in the Divine image, how we are made to be mirrors of essential grace.

The journey of the spirit through the domes is a journey of recognition, as the spirit discovers the hidden parts of itself, the spiritual archetypes hidden within its form. On the previous stair the individual learned to understand unity from an external, universal perspective, discovering the purpose and origin of the universe in love. On this stage of the journey, the spirit discovers a more internal understanding of unity, and of its origin in grace. Through the recognition and integration of its archetypes, the spirit understands that its journey home is to a unified point, a point of original grace.

On this last step of the return journey the spirit may stop at any stage and remain within one of the turning rings of grace. This ring will reflect their own spiritual nature, and its ray will be one that resonates with their human personality. Some spirits, however, pass through each of the rings without resting, fuelled by attractive desire for their ultimate source. These spirits reach the innermost dome, and a few of them travel beyond it, passing through the window of grace, to reach their final destination.

WINDOWS IN THE OUTER DOME OF GRACE

The Window of Transcendence

The Window of Illumination

The Window of Unified Life

THE WINDOW OF TRANSCENDENCE

The spirit is carried by a turning pillar of flame upwards into the outer dome of grace. Looking up the spirit sees rings of coloured light, leading upwards and inwards. Looking around, it sees other spirits, turning in graceful flight. The inner note of each spirit resounds in harmony with the others, and the spirit finds itself resounding also, with the note of its own inner song. Looking at itself it sees that its form is no longer dense, but a mosaic of different coloured lights moving together in harmony.

A TRANSCENDENT CONNECTION

A column of flame connects the spirit to the fire of friendship below. The spirit is always connected to the fire wherever it travels in the domes of grace. As the spirit rises this pillar becomes a thin cord of light. This cord anchors the spirit to the realm of humanity, and to the fire of friendship, the fire that it chose for love's sake.

This link is important because the beauty of the domes is such that it would be easy to forget how you got there, if you were not reminded through your connection to the fire. This connection ensures that the individual who travels in spirit through the domes does not get bewildered by their experiences, but remains balanced and grounded in their life in a material body on earth.

The friends in the fire remind the individual that they are not special, but just like everyone and everything else, on a voyage of return to their essence. In this way the individual whose consciousness travels through the domes is helped to understand that the domes of grace are an introduction to a state of being that we will all one day experience.

THE PURPOSE OF THE JOURNEY

Within the turning column of flame the spirit realises the true nature of transcendence. To transcend is to rise above, to go beyond. It sees that it has risen above and gone beyond the path it previously followed, that it is no longer climbing a staircase, but rising effortlessly through the rooftop domes. It sees that this transcendence happened because it understood the purpose of the

spiritual journey, its true point. It understood that to become unconditionally loving is the purpose of the path; it realised this through
its own experience, through its choice to burn in the fire for love.

Through choosing to burn in the fire the spirit has transcended the
temporal and spatial reality of material being. It has become a free
spirit, timeless and placeless. The death of the material body holds
no fear for the transcendent spirit. The individual has transcended
their own death, as they understand that the energy of their spirit
cannot die, that it is always living in one form or another.

The spirit also understands that the journey will always
continue, because pure universal love always continues. There is
no point where it ends, for it is constantly expressing itself. The
spirit understands that in the domes it will begin to deeply
appreciate the attributes of universal love expressed through the
rings of grace. It will draw nearer to their starting point, the point
where love always is, a point of original grace.

THE RING OF TRANSCENDENCE

As the spirit realises the transcendent nature of its own journey, the
column of flame in which it rests expands to become an orange gold
ring. The spirit is still connected to the fire below by a thin cord of light,
but the column itself spreads out to form a ring in the lowest dome.

Although the spirit has its own integrity and holds together as a
separate being, it is also able to merge its form with the light of the
different coloured rings that revolve around the domes. In this way
it is able to absorb the essence of each ring, and understand each
one's attributes and symbols.

THE SYMBOL OF TRANSCENDENCE

Within the orange ring the spirit loses its form and assimilates
the energy of this ring. It understands that the symbol of
transcendence is a pillar of flame that both rises above and falls
below. This pillar is a symbol of connection, the connection of all
being to its own transcendent source. The spirit feels its own sense
of connection to this source, and realises that its own evolution
contributes to the evolution of the whole. All being is returning to
source, and as our connection becomes illumined we assist the
evolutionary journey of all life.

As it realises that its own evolution aids that of the whole the spirit experiences great joy and lightness of being. It understands that its further progress through the domes will be a banquet of the lights of grace, and that this nourishment is what it needs to grow in strength, illumination and understanding. It has come home.

Filled with joy the spirit starts to turn around, and this movement is mirrored by the turning of the orange ring. As the ring turns it rises and expands, and changes colour from orange to gold. The spirit now finds itself in a ring of yellow gold light that is turning in the outer dome of grace. This is the ring of illumination.

THE RAY OF TRANSCENDENCE
The window of transcendence is a large arched opening in the outer dome of grace. A ray of orange light shines through this window to the levels below.

If this ray touches you, a feeling of transcendent grace will lift you out of the reality you are accustomed to, into a transcendent reality, the reality of this light. A transcendent experience can happen to you at any time. The hallmark of such an experience is that it changes your perception of what is important, and makes you aware of the spiritual side of your being. This light awakens your slumbering spirit, enabling you to rise above yourself and review your life and its meaning. It can revolutionise your understanding of the purpose behind illness, loss and change; it is a liberating light, for it helps you find the spiritual lesson hidden in all experience.

THE ANGELS OF THE RAYS OF GRACE
The angels of the rays of grace travel with the rays down to earth, to assist in the enlightenment of humanity. They are not the same as the spirits in the domes, who have had human lifetimes. The angels have always lived in the domes; they have always existed in pure consciousness without material form. Each ray has angels who assist in the process of helping the energy of the rings of grace to descend. The angels of the rays have specific places on earth that they visit. Here they illumine and spiritually nourish those who are most in need of the grace of their particular ray.

THE ANGELS OF TRANSCENDENCE

The angels of this ray bring the orange light of transcendence and sacred celebration. They are found in holy places, on sacred sites and in consecrated buildings. They exist to help the human spirit transcend its everyday limitations, and to help sincere aspirants of every spiritual tradition to experience the transcendent nature of grace. They help people to lift their consciousness above the material realm, to experience true freedom of spirit. If you have a room in your house that you use for prayer and meditation, you can attract an angel of this ray, through an attitude of reverence and sincere aspiration. It is to this leaning of the human spirit that they respond.

THE GENEROSITY OF THE RAYS OF GRACE

The rays of grace falling from the windows in the domes want to help you see clearly, to help you understand, to help you grow. The angels of each ray want to touch you, to bless you. This is the generous nature of grace. You do not have to go through the fire of friendship to receive the blessing of the rays of grace and their angels. The rays fall on the whole of creation, through the windows of their names, and they help the whole to evolve. All you have to do to receive their grace is to ask for them with sincerity, and then open up as they descend.

RECEIVING THE BLESSING OF THE RAYS OF GRACE

If you would like to receive the blessing of the rays of grace, you can ask for them in your own way, using your own words. The instructions set out in the chapters below are for any who are unsure how to ask for themselves; I demonstrate one method of asking for the rays, and explain how to receive their blessing. If you have trouble following these instructions, do not worry. Just repeat the invocations, focus on the ray and its particular colour, and see it shining down on you from a ring above your head. You will receive the benefit of each ray as it descends. You do not actively have to do anything, except ask and receive.

The exercises to help you receive the rays of grace are presented in three stages. It is better to become familiar with the first stage before proceeding to stage two. Stage two involves a deeper reception of each rays light, through receiving the blessing of its ring. Only the rays that issue from the innermost dome have a third stage to their reception. This stage is for those who are comfortable with stage one and two, and who would like to receive the blessing of the communion of the rings of grace.

There are also instructions given on how to share the rays of grace with another person, or with a group of people who would benefit from their light. Further instructions on the group receptions are given at the end of the book.

HOW TO GROUND AND CENTRE THE BODY BEFORE RECEIVING THE RAYS OF GRACE

Before you ask the rays to descend, there are a few initial preparations that will help you to relax, and to become well grounded and centred. These will ensure that the spiritual influence of each ray becomes anchored in your body, so that its beneficial vibration will remain with you when the meditation is over.

Find a quiet space and time where you will not be disturbed for at least half an hour. Sit comfortably on a chair or on the floor. Allow your body and mind to relax. If it helps you to relax, you can imagine yourself in a favourite place in the natural world, somewhere beautiful and peaceful.

Become aware of your breathing. Allow your body to relax more deeply as you breathe more deeply.

Imagine two roots coming out of the soles of your feet and going deep into the ground, connecting you to the centre of the earth. Imagine a large taproot descending from the base of your spine, to connect you with the centre of the earth.

Imagine the energy of the earth coming up your 'roots' and holding you firmly. Feel a deep sense of connection to the ground. Feel the heartbeat of the earth beneath you, let yourself breathe with the earth. Let your breath flow down your roots, into the earth.

Bring the earth's energy up your feet and legs to gather at a point at the base of your spine. Then focus on your centre. Focus on a warm ball of light at your navel. Breathe into this point. Feel the stability of your centre.

Be aware of what it is like to feel relaxed, grounded and centred. Be aware of this feeling, so that at the end of the exercises you can ground and centre yourself again, if you need to.

THE RECEPTION OF THE RAY OF TRANSCENDENCE

When you are ready to receive the ray of transcendence, repeat the following invocation (to yourself, or out aloud):

"May I receive the grace of the orange ray of transcendence. May the angels of transcendence please be with me."

Visualise a ring of orange light one foot above the crown of your head. This ring should be about one foot in diameter. From the ring let a ray of orange light descend, down to your crown. Let the ray of grace enter your body at a point on the top of your head, at your crown. Allow this ray to flow down the back of your head, down your neck, down your spine, down your legs and into the earth through your feet. Let it also flow out of your body from the base of your spine straight down into the earth. Allow yourself to feel your connection to the earth and to the sky. Let this transcendent ray anchor you to the earth, as it brings you the grace of heaven.

You may be aware of an angelic presence in the room. Whether you sense them with you or not, the energy of the angels is always loving, uplifting and healing.

Then bring the orange ray back up your spine, up your neck and then let orange light fill your head. Feel its ray behind your closed eyelids. If you have a particular problem that you want to solve, or if you want a new way of looking at an old pattern, ask this ray to help you transcend your limited view. In your mind's eye visualise your problem, your repetitive pattern, or the situation that you don't understand. Let the mental picture you have made of your problem be suffused with orange light. Fill your mind with the energy of this ray, and then look at your mental picture again. Allow this ray to bring you its transcendent wisdom.

The light of transcendent grace will help you see the truth behind your repetitive pattern, or dilemma. It may give you a word, a symbol, or a picture to help you see this truth. It may give you a feeling. The energy of this ray will help you see in a new way. It will not give you neat answers to your problems, for this would not really help you. The light of transcendence will lift your consciousness so that you will be able to see for yourself the lessons that your life is trying to teach you. Then you will be able to make your own solutions, or realise that no solutions are necessary. You will receive the healing hidden in the lesson.

GIVING THANKS FOR THE RAYS AND THEIR ANGELS
This is the end of the first stage. When you are ready let the orange ray pass out through your crown, back to the ring above your head. As you send it back repeat:

"I thank the ray of transcendence for the light of its grace."

Being grateful helps you to develop gracefully. It helps you not to take the rays and their angels for granted, even though they descend on you freely.

As the energy of the orange ray leaves you, bring your attention back to your body. Breathe deeply and make sure you are firmly rooted to the ground. Feel the roots in your feet and tailbone holding you securely. Find your centre at your navel. Breathe deeply into this centre. Then when you are ready to do so, open your eyes. After receiving any of the rays, make sure you are grounded and centred before coming back to everyday consciousness.

When you have done the first stage a few times and feel comfortable with it, you can move on to stage two, if you wish.

THE DEEPER RECEPTION OF THE RAY OF TRANSCENDENCE
After having done the first stage of the exercise, do not send the orange ray back to the ring above your head. Instead let it travel down your neck and spine to a point opposite your navel.
Then repeat:

"May I receive the deeper grace of the orange ray of transcendence.
May I feel the blessing of its ring."

Bring the orange ray forward from your spine to rest in a point that is in the centre of your body. Then let the orange light radiate outwards in a ring from this point. Let it radiate out in a ring two feet in front of you and two feet behind you. Feel the radiation of this ring of grace that has come to you from a transcendent ray. Rest in your own ring of transcendent grace. As you breathe let your ring contract and expand inwards and outwards from its central point. As the ring radiates outwards, allow yourself to feel the healing power of your own sun. As it contracts inwards allow yourself to feel the healing power of your own joyful point. Breathe deeply as it expands and contracts, and then expand the ring and hold it still.

As you breathe you may like to repeat a word, a word that sums up the essence of this rings light. For the ring of transcendence this word is 'Joy'. As you repeat this word silently to the rhythm of your breath, feel the joy of a transcendent blessing. Feel the influence of the angels of the orange ray, those who come to share this blessing with you. You may sense an angelic presence behind you, holding your shoulders. Through the blessing of this ring you experience a connection of joy, through a transcendent orange ray which becomes a ring within your own being.

GIVING THANKS FOR THE DEEPER RECEPTION OF THE RAY OF TRANSCENDENCE
When you are ready to come out of the meditation let the ring of orange light contract to a point at your centre. Take this point to your spine, and then send the ray up your back, neck and head, to the place at your crown where it entered. Send it back up to the ring above you and as it is leaving you, repeat:

"I thank the ray of transcendence for the blessing of its ring."

Make sure you are grounded and centred before you open your eyes.

REMEMBRANCE OF THE BLESSING OF THE RINGS OF GRACE
You can remember the blessing of this ring and its angels throughout your day. Remember this ring as with your breath you remember its joyful expansion and contraction. You can repeat the word 'Joy' to yourself whenever you feel like remembering it. You can remember the blessing of an angel standing behind you, holding you within a ring of grace.

Our being is a mirror for the domes of grace. We contain this treasury within ourselves. Be grateful for the blessing of the rings of grace, as you understand that they belong in your own being, for heaven is where you are. We contain all the wisdom, power and love expressed by the rays and their angels. The reason we connect to them without is to help us remember their presence within. So remember the blessing of the orange ring of grace, a blessing of transcendent joy. As you remember this ring, you will receive its subtle healing influence, in a way that will gently purify your being and illumine your consciousness.

THE WINDOW OF ILLUMINATION

The spirit carried by the expansion of the orange ring, finds itself turning in a ring of golden light, the ring of illumination. Within this ring the spirit begins to assimilate a deeper understanding of its own light. This understanding illumines its awareness, making clear and lucid that which was previously hidden from view.

THE SYMBOL OF ILLUMINATION

Losing its form in the light of the golden ring, the spirit understands that the symbol of illumination is a candle that never goes out. It understands that its own journey has been aided by the light of this candle, a light it has received through the medium of others, and also directly from the source. It understands that this light is the same as the one it carries within, its own essential light. However, when it was younger it didn't always understand this, and looked to the light of others to help it find its way. It understands that the journey towards grace involves the recognition of its own inner light, which becomes its true guide.

The spirit understands that this light can be shared, as it loses its form and tastes the illumined essence of this ring. The spirit loses all sense of separation, and experiences a communion of illumined grace.

SPIRITUAL ENLIGHTENMENT

The spirit realises that the divine light is eternal because it remains alive through different vessels in different times, and that it is universal because it is latent in every being, however hidden. It sees that spiritual enlightenment is not about discovering something new, but about uncovering what is already there. Each successive stage of its path has been a stage of discarding or aligning layers that blocked its inner light. Now in the domes of grace the spirit sees that this light always inspired it to go on, to discard or align the layers that distorted its perception of its true self.

The spirit knows that finding your way home begins when you have the first inkling of a spark within that can lead you to a more graceful way of being. It realises that all the steps it had to take, and all the years of struggle, were because it had many layers to discard or align before it could have complete faith and trust in its own essential light.

CLAIMING YOUR SPIRITUAL INHERITANCE

To uncover your essential light is to uncover within a legacy of grace, the spiritual inheritance of Adam and Eve, a wealth of light that belongs to us all. The spirit understands that this inheritance is one that we are given to share, as through our light others are helped to recognise theirs. The spirit that claims its own spiritual inheritance accepts the responsibility inherent in the recovery of its light, a responsibility to shine as a candle, and share the blessing of illuminative grace. This blessing is one that spreads light, dispelling shadows of doubt and despair. The illumination grace radiates always brings hope and peace, as it helps people find their way.

Here in the domes of grace, the spirit is nearer to its source, the source of its illumination, the original point of its light. It is this source that is attracting the spirit to return, pulling the spirit gently towards itself, on a journey through the turning rings of grace. At this stage the golden ring begins to rise and to expand. As it moves upwards and outwards, the gold ring turns green. The spirit now finds itself turning in a ring of emerald green light, the ring of unified life.

THE RAY OF ILLUMINED GRACE

Light from the ring of illumination falls down to earth through the window of this name. It touches anyone who has ever had an experience of illuminative grace. This ray helps you find your way; it reaches you when you are lost in despair. It brings you a taste of grace, as you feel the direction and hope that its light brings.

It is not only in moments of desperation that you receive the blessing of this ray. You can receive it in moments of illumined vision when an inner flame lights your understanding. You receive it when your higher intellect sees through inessentials, to grasp the illumined thread of truth. But it is in moments of despair, when you are lost, that you fully appreciate the grace of its ray.

THE ANGELS OF ILLUMINATION

The angels of this ray are those who bring the golden light of hope and illumined understanding. They descend in hopeless places where there is brutality, ignorance and suicidal despair. They can be found in institutions, in prisons, in reformatories, in mental hospitals. The golden angels of illumination travel on the rays of grace down to the pockets of hell where people are most lost, for this is where they are most needed. And here they bring the candle of this ray to any that are crying out for light.

They also visit those who struggle to know, those who seek clear vision and understanding of truth. Those who are sincere in their quest for true knowledge are inspired and assisted by the angels of this ray.

RECEPTION OF THE RAY OF ILLUMINED GRACE

Follow the instructions at the end of the book for relaxing, grounding and centring the body.

When you are ready to receive this ray, use the following invocation:

"May I receive the grace of the golden ray of illumination.
May the angels of illumination please be with me."

Then feel a yellow gold beam of light falling down on you from a golden ring above your head. This golden ring should be about one foot above the crown of your head, and one foot in diameter. Let the ray enter your body at your crown. Bring it down your head, neck and spine, and then let it flow down your legs, and down the base of your spine into the earth. Then bring the golden ray back up your spine to a point opposite your heart centre. Bring it forward, so that it fills your heart centre with light. Your heart centre, or heart chakra, is a centre of subtle energy that is in the middle of your upper chest. Bring the ray into this centre, and let your heart warm up as it holds this rays light. Then in your heart centre visualise a candle burning, symbol of illumination, of illumined grace. Know that this candle will never go out, that it always has, and always will, illumine your soul's path.

THE ASSISTANCE OF AN ANGEL OF ILLUMINATION

You may feel the presence of an angel of illumination standing in front of you. If you do, receive their blessing, as you let them hold you in their arms. As you do so you will feel another ray of light falling from the ring above you to hold your outer body in its beam. Accept the illumination of the golden ray, as it gives you its warmth, peace and illumined vision. Inhale deeply the golden light of this ray.

THE ASSISTANCE OF THE RAY OF ILLUMINATION

Allow the ray of illumination within to feed the candle in your heart. As you feel it feeding your inner light let the flame in your heart centre burn bright and strong. Through this light let yourself be assisted and guided. If you are in despair, ask this light to help you. Ask it to show you a way out, to help you see the thread of light that leads to a new beginning. Even if your circumstances, health, or upbringing have caused you much pain, ask to see the way to understand your experience, and the way to grow beyond it. Ask for clarity and illumination about any situation in which you feel helpless or trapped.

If you are a victim of addiction, ask to find a way out of your present situation. Ask for light, for hope, for strength and for support. Just as there are energies that take you down and lead you into self destructive patterns of living, so there are energies that help you rise, and lead you to find more positive ways to live and grow. The angels and their rays are a form of positive energy that descends to help us find our way home. Let them help you find your way.

This ray will help you see the way out of impossible situations, relationships you must leave, jobs you must change. It will help you see which relationships and occupations will assist your growth and healing. It will reveal to you that which your innermost heart already knows, it will illumine the knowledge you already have. We know deep down which situations are preventing our growth. The light of illumination clarifies this, so that we have the confidence to act on our intuition. This candle shows us our true situation, and then holds us in its light, so that we may draw strength, hope and courage from it, and feel supported with every new step.

When you have received enough of this light, send the golden ray up your spine, then up your neck and head, and out through your crown. As you send it back to the ring above you, say:

" I thank the ray of illumination for the candle of its grace."

Make sure you are grounded and centred before you open your eyes.

THE DEEPER RECEPTION OF THE RAY OF ILLUMINED GRACE
Once you have become familiar with the first part of the exercise, you can proceed to stage two, and receive the deeper illumination of this ray.

Do not send the golden ray back to its ring, but let it continue to illumine your heart. Focus on the candle in your heart, fed by this ray's light. Then say:

"May I feel the deeper grace of the golden ray of illumination.
May I feel the blessing of its ring."

Focus on the point of light inside your heart where the candle's flame is burning. From this point, let golden light expand outwards in a ring. Let this ring spread out from your heart centre to two feet in front of you, and two feet behind you.

With your breath be aware of the contraction and expansion of this illumined ring around the heart. As you breathe in let the golden ring contract to a point in the candle's flame. As you breathe out let the golden ring expand, as you radiate outwards the illumination of your inner light. As you breathe you might like to silently repeat the word 'Light', to the steady rhythm of your breath.

As you repeat the word 'Light', allow the ring to remain extended two feet from your body, so that it no longer contracts with your inward breath. Let the golden ring remain still. Within this still ring of grace feel the protection of the light of grace. Feel surrounded by the loving, positive energy of the universe, which is blessing you in a ring. You may feel invisible hands on your shoulders inside the ring, the hands of an angel, protective and strong. You may just feel a loving energy all around you. Be aware that wherever you are, and whatever you are doing, the protection of this ring is available to you. You can remember this ring, its loving protection and its light, with every breath. It can surround you through the busy hours of your day, and fill you with its love, its hope and its strength.

When you have received enough light and hope from the golden ring let it contract to a point in your heart, the point of your candle's flame. Send the golden point to your spine, then up your back and neck, and out of your head at the crown. As you send it back to the ring above your head, remember to say:

" I thank the ray of illumination for the blessing of its ring."

Make sure you are grounded and centred before you open your eyes.

SHARING THIS RING WITH ANOTHER PERSON
If you are with someone who is lost and desperate, you can call upon the healing light of this ring to help them find their way. Remember the invocation and the colour of the ray. When you get to stage two, repeat (to yourself, if you prefer):

"May we feel the deeper grace of the golden ray of illumination.
May we feel the blessing of its ring.
May the angels of illumination please be with us."

You can ask the angels of this ray to support you and the person you are with. As you create the ring around your heart, let it extend to hold them in its light also. Let it extend to about four feet around you both. Within a ring of illumined grace you will both be protected from fear and despair. If you trust this ring to protect you and others, it will.

THE SPIRITUAL ESSENCE OF THE RING OF ILLUMINATION
The light of the ring of illumination gives you hope. It helps you to feel the positive energy behind creation. You can feel this positive energy through the love, strength and hope that comes to you from this golden ring. You may also feel this loving energy through the touch of an angel standing behind you. The touch of the angels always brings light, hope and peace.

The ring of golden light that surrounds your heart in the second stage of this exercise is a ring of protection. It will protect you from your own despair. It is a ring of power, for the light of this ring dispels fear, and fills you with the light of hope. It is a ring you can turn to in emergencies, a ring you can use in your daily life if you need it.

HOW TO RECEIVE THIS RAY IF YOU DON'T BELIEVE IN IT

If you are held back from asking for the lights of grace because you don't believe in them, or believe that they can help you, you can ask for help with your disbelief. Even though you may want and need them, you may feel that there is no point in asking, because you can't ask in the right spirit. If you are insincere you cannot receive anything, because you have not really asked. But if you are sincere, even about your lack of faith, help will come. If you don't believe in the ray of illumined grace, and don't believe it can help you, but you need help all the same, just say:

> *" Ray of illumined grace if you are there please help me.*
> *Angels of illumination, if you can hear me, please be with me. "*

You will open a door to the ray if you ask like this, even if you don't believe in it. This ray will fall on you, for it wants to help you. It wants to help you move beyond where you are, out of a trap, out of despair. The rays of grace and their angels are conscious, they have consciousness. They are not impersonal. They care about each and every one of us, whether or not we believe in them. For we are all part of the whole, as they are, and our evolution is part of theirs.

THE WINDOW OF UNIFIED LIFE

The spirit now finds itself in a wide ring of emerald green light that is turning in the outer dome of grace. Other spirits are turning in this ring and the new spirit joins them, turning in the emerald light. As the spirit assimilates the energy of this ring, it begins to understand how grace brings life and vitality to all being.

THE SYMBOL OF THE RING OF LIFE

As it drinks this light, the spirit sees that the symbol of this ring is a fountain that never runs dry. It sees the continuity of all life, the constancy of living things that turn in cycles of birth, death, and rebirth. It understands that just as the natural world runs in cycles, so does spiritual growth, as our evolution is cyclical in nature. It sees all life rising and falling in a fountain, and sees its own lifetimes as part of this pattern. Here in the ring of life it finds itself at the fountainhead, receiving the grace that sustains all life. It understands that its spirit has always been sustained by this living energy whatever its form.

THE TAPESTRY OF CREATION

In the ring of life the spirit understands how the kingdoms of nature express the beauty and healing quality of this ring. The spirit understands that all life is beautiful, even those forms that may at first seem ugly or dangerous. Their beauty lies in the fact that they have a place in the whole, they fit within the tapestry of creation. They all originate in a harmonious ring, and their essence holds the memory of this perfect state. Rocks and stones, plants and trees, insect life, birds, fish, animals, human kind, discarnate guides and teachers, hold the imprint of this light within, and have their unique part to play in the formation of the whole.

The spirit understands that all forms of life have their own contribution to make to creation, and that all have within them healing properties, properties that serve the whole. All the natural kingdoms, animal, vegetable and mineral, have something to share with humanity, and can help us heal our sense of alienation from the whole. Humankind has the intelligence to recognise and use these properties, to heal its ills, and accelerate its evolution. The spirit understands that it is the energy of these forms of life that can be used for planetary and individual healing. This healing energy is the light it drinks in the emerald ring in the outer dome, a ring of life giving energy that has not yet been distilled into form.

THE EVOLUTION OF CONSCIOUSNESS

The spirit in the ring understands that the form all being takes depends upon its level of consciousness. It sees that at its least conscious this energy manifests as dense matter, in stones and rock. As it becomes more conscious its form evolves into vegetable and then animal life. We have all been minerals, plants and animals at some stage in our evolution, and this knowledge causes the spirit to feel tenderness for all life, as it feels its connection to it. All natural form carries within it the energy of living grace, and the strength, beauty and harmony of the natural world reflect its graceful essence.

AN EXPANDED EXPRESSION OF THE POINT OF UNITY

As the spirit revolves within the emerald ring, it understands that this ring is an expression of the dynamic energy of unity. The point of unity (also called the point of truth) is a point in the upper-most innermost dome, from which the rings of grace expand as they descend. The ring of life is the most expanded expression of this point. It is the widest ring in all three domes, the rings below it and above it are all smaller. The ring of life expresses outwardly the creative essence of the point of unity. This ring is the spiritual blueprint for the circle of life that the individual embraced on the stair below, at the step of unity. The spirit now assimilates the spiritual essence of this circle, as it merges with the green ring. This ring, as an expanded expression of the point of unity, has both a horizontal and a vertical dimension.

THE VERTICAL DIMENSION OF THIS RING

Vertically energy descends from this ring downwards through many levels of being to manifest on the material plane as dense matter. The spiritual journey of all life is to ascend from the densest manifestation of this light upwards to its most diffuse manifestation. This most diffuse manifestation is where the spirit now finds itself, mingling and merging as it assimilates the refreshment of this rings of light.

THE HORIZONTAL DIMENSION OF THIS RING

The hierarchy of creation, however, only exists from a vertical perspective. The horizontal aspect of this ring affirms the equality and interdependence of all life. The ring spreads out horizontally to unite all life from the purest intelligence to the heaviest stone, in a circle of brotherhood. All are held in this ring in a horizontal sense in absolute equality, as all life material and spiritual is held in common through the living energy that manifests through it.

THE HUMAN BEING AS THE MIRROR OF CREATION

The individual whose spirit travels through the domes experiences again their relatedness, their brother and sisterhood with all life, as they did at the stage of trust, of patience, and of friendship, but this time with greater understanding. Within this ring the spirit understands why the human being is the mirror of all created life. A human being stands between earth and heaven, and mediates between the two. A human being is able to reflect light down to the realms of matter through which they passed on their vertical journey of ascent. He or she is also able to receive light from above, from the guides and angelic intelligences in the spiritual realm, who have passed beyond (or never been embodied in) dense form. The human being is then able to stand in the middle of the circle, and affirm the purpose of creation on all levels, as they mirror its central point, a point of universal love.

The point of creation is mirrored in a human heart that has understood its connection to the whole, and realised its purpose in universal love. The human being is a mirror for all life above and below, and is able to unite the vertical and horizontal aspects of the ring of unity in a point in their own being. Turning in the ring of life, the spirit accepts its connection to all life, and understands its central place in the scheme of creation. It understands that its family includes everything alive, and that it has a responsibility to cherish and support all its relations.

THE BLESSING OF ETERNAL LIFE

The spirit also realises again, at the deepest level of its being, its oneness with all life. There is no separation between our essence, and the essence of everything else alive on any level. In truth there is no separation; there is only the energy of life that all of us express whether incarnate or discarnate. This energy cannot die, just as the still point within us cannot die. We can all partake of the blessing of eternal life, if we become conscious enough to find its point within ourselves.

THE INNER DOME

In the outer dome of grace the spirit drinks its fill of the emerald light and understands the healing grace hidden in all life. Enraptured by the beauty of this ring the spirit feels the overflowing generosity of creation. As it does so it finds the ring of green light gently contracting, and moving with the ring it finds itself being propelled upwards and inwards, into the next dome. The spirit now finds itself in a ring of rose pink light that is turning in the inner dome of grace, the ring of abundant blessing.

THE RAY OF UNIFIED LIFE

The energy of the ring of life is found in all created form, but it also descends in an individual ray from a window in the outer dome, the window of unified life.

The effect of the ray of life is to enliven and sustain. It both creates, and helps whatever it has created to stay alive. So whether it is the birth of a child, the birth of an idea or creative project, the creation of a garden, or the birth of a relationship, the energy of this ring will help whatever you create to flourish and grow.

As well as being creative, this ray has a deeply healing quality. It heals through bringing balance and harmony. It is a ray that brings you back into balance, as you begin to connect again with your own inner source of vitality and health. It can balance your physical body, your emotions, your mental state, and your relationships with others. It radiates the healing energy that sustains life, an energy that is nourishing and benign.

THE ANGELS OF LIFE

The angels of this ray bring the emerald green light of unity and creativity. They are found in the natural world, in the countryside, in woods and fields, beside waterfalls and streams, in gardens and parkland. If you have a garden you can attract the angels of this ray, by sensitive care for the life of all beings in your green space. The angels of this ray respond to those who care for life in all its forms. They refresh the spirits of all who come to nature in order to revive and heal. The angels of the emerald ray bring harmony to those who are tired and dispirited, out of balance with their environment, and out of tune with themselves.

RECEPTION OF THE RAY OF UNIFIED LIFE

If you would like to feel a ray of living, unifying grace in your life, you can ask for it. You do not have to go to the natural world to attract its angels; you can feel this ray in the middle of the city, if you take a little time to receive it silently.

Follow the instructions at the end of the book for relaxing, grounding and centring your body before you ask the ray to descend.

When you are ready to receive it, repeat:

> *"May I receive the grace of the emerald ray of life.*
> *May the angels of life please be with me."*

Imagine a ring of emerald light about one foot above your head. Let a ray descend from this ring, onto a point at your crown. Receive the emerald light. Bring it down from your head, down your neck and spine, and into the earth beneath you. Then bring it back up the spine to a point which is opposite your navel. Bring it forward from here to a point that is half way between your navel and your spine, a point at the centre of your body. Feel your own centre here, your centre of balance.

You may feel the presence of an angel standing in front of you. Let them hold you as you receive another ray from the ring above your head, a ray that envelops your outer body in its beam. Breathe in the emerald light.

Then let the emerald ray at your centre crystallise into an emerald stone, radiating green light. Let emerald light radiate from the stone at your centre. Let this stone become a spring of green, pouring forth cascades of emerald light. Let this fountain of green light fill your whole body. Let light flow into your stomach, up your chest, down your arms to your hands, and up your neck to your head. Let it flow down your abdomen and down your legs to your feet.

Feel yourself bathed internally by the green light flowing from an emerald stone at your centre. Drink the healing radiance of this light, which brings all into harmony and balance. Give it all your weariness, and feel it gradually bringing you back to life. Let this light bathe the parts of you that you have cut off and denied, the parts of you that you no longer want to own. Receive the whole of yourself, as this light integrates you on all levels. Feel yourself returning to equilibrium. The emerald ray is a ray of unifying living grace. It will bring you back into balance, and help you regain your vitality and your sense of wholeness.

When you have received enough of this light let your inner fountain contract to the emerald stone at your centre. Treasure this jewel as you repeat:

" I thank the ray of unified life for the fountain of its grace."

Make sure you are grounded and centred before you open your eyes.

THE DEEPER RECEPTION OF THE RAY OF UNIFIED LIFE
When you are ready you can proceed to stage two. Contract the fountain of green light to the emerald stone at your centre, then repeat:

" May I receive the deeper grace of the emerald ray of life.
May I feel the blessing of its ring."

From the stone at your centre let a green ring radiate outwards, two feet in front of you and two feet behind you. As you breathe in let the ring contract to the emerald at your centre; as you breathe out let the ring expand. After you have breathed in this way for a little while, extend the ring and let it become still. Cease to contract it as you breathe in. Repeat the word 'Harmony' to yourself, in rhythm with your breath, for this is the healing essence of this ring. Feel held and supported by the emerald energy of a living ring that surrounds you, feel held in its embrace.

Then remember the emerald green ring of light above your head from which the ray of life descended. Slowly and deliberately bring this ring down from above your head, to meet and merge with the ring that encircles your body. Let the ring above you expand as you bring it down, so that it is the right size to merge with the ring that surrounds you. This is easier to do than it sounds. As the rings meet in harmony, let yourself breathe in the same way. Be aware that you do not have to strain to receive the rings of grace, that they can easily come to you. Feel your connection to the earth beneath you and the sky above you. Feel how both earth and heaven meet at your centre, that this is your point of balance.

As you breathe in balance let the emerald ring around you slowly begin to turn. Let it turn to the right. Turn the ring of life, as you sit motionless inside it. As it turns let it return you to health. Let it bring you the energy of the emerald ray, the ray that creates, the ray that encourages new life. Let it bring you the creative energy of grace, that is an eternal resurrection. Let it give you the energy you need to feel well, to feel new, to be born again. And as the ring turns let it return you to wholeness, the wholeness we find in everything new born. Let it return you to yourself, your true self that is whole. Feel held by the slowly turning ring in perfect balance.

When you have received enough of the healing grace of the emerald ring, let it slow down and become still. Then contract it to the emerald jewel at your centre. Let this jewel remain within you, do not send it back to the ring above your head. As you focus on the jewel at your centre, say:

" I thank the ray of unified life for the blessing of its ring."

Make sure you are well grounded before you open your eyes.

SHARING THIS RING WITH ANOTHER PERSON

If you are with someone else who is seriously exhausted or out of balance, you can ask for the healing of this ring for them. You can also do this for children or animals who are exhausted or disturbed. If they are well enough you should ask for their permission to do this; if not always ask as you create the ring that this healing be in their best interests.

Once you have asked that the healing be in their best interests, go through stage one. When you get to stage two, say:

*" May we receive the deeper grace of the emerald ray of life.
May we feel the blessing of its ring. May the angels of life please be with us."*

When you form your ring allow it to spread out from your centre to encircle both of you. Let the emerald light encircle you both, to extend four feet around you. Then bring down the ring above you to meet and merge with the ring that encircles you both. Let it adjust its size to fit the ring you have created. As the rings meet, ask for balance for both you and the other person. You can also ask the angels of this ray to support you both. Feel the energy of the ring encircling you, as emerald angels hold you.

THE SPIRITUAL ESSENCE OF THIS RING
The emerald ring that you bring down in the previous meditation is a reflection of the true ring of life that exists in the higher ethers. Although it is a reflection, it carries the same energy, and the same healing qualities.
　　Whether your imbalance is primarily physical, mental or emotional, the healing vibration of this light will both bring you into harmony, and help you understand why you were out of tune. It will bring you back into balance through the vibration of its ring, a ring that resonates with your own being. Your own vital energy will respond to the chord that reminds it of its source in a ring of living grace. This memory will initiate healing, as your subtle bodies will respond to the harmonious vibration of their source.

HOW TO SHARE THE RINGS OF GRACE
Although being conscious of the rings essence helps you to understand the benefit you receive from them, those who are not conscious of the rings will benefit just as much from their healing energy. Children, animals and the very sick can all be helped to receive a healing ray of living grace. The rays of grace are for everyone, and in your life always be ready to share that which you have received. Always do this for free, not for material reward. Give generously, with love, and then your giving will echo the generosity of the rings themselves.

WINDOWS IN THE INNER DOME OF GRACE

The Window of Abundant Blessing

The Window of Compassionate Peace

The Window of Sacred Healing

THE WINDOW OF ABUNDANT BLESSING

The emerald ring carries the spirit upwards and inwards into the inner dome of grace. Here it finds itself turning in a rose pink ring, the ring of abundant blessing. This ring is a delicate rose pink and has a delicious fragrance, a sweet scent of roses. In the ring of abundant blessing the spirit understands that grace falls freely like the rain, sending showers of blessing down to all.

THE TRUE NATURE OF BLESSING

In the rose pink ring the spirit realises the true nature of blessing. A blessing is an outpouring of grace, a breath of benevolent light. Here in the rings of grace, close to its source, the spirit is closer to the origin of all blessing, the point from which blessing issues forth. It issues forth from the point of grace that was never born and will never die. The breath of the Divine point always is, it doesn't begin or end. It is blessed because its motivation is lovingly creative; it breathes forth creation as a blessing. This is a blessing anyone can experience, as they breathe in gratitude for their life.

Breathing in gratitude, the spirit experiences the celebration of grace. It understands that life is a celebration, a celebration of love made manifest. Everything living is able to celebrate the joy of being alive, but the more conscious it is, the more it understands the true source of this joy. We celebrate our source, as we recognise that we are an expression of the Divine Breath, and that God celebrates His Life through us. The spirit in the inner dome breathes in gratitude for the blessing of this ring, and for the grace of the point that first conceived it.

A CONNECTION OF ABUNDANT GRACE

At this stage the spirit merges into the energy of the rose coloured ring, and loses its individual form. It experiences a connection of abundant grace, a connection to a line of grace that spans the ages. This line of grace connects the spirit to the spiritual legacy of all of those who blessed creation with their breath. Humanity has always been able to access this inheritance, through the medium of individuals who connected them to it. In every age there are those who provide a channel for this line of grace, who bring down the rain of blessing for the rest.

THE ROBE OF BLESSING

The spirit in the inner dome returns to itself to find that it is wearing a robe of shimmering coloured light. This robe sparkles with the colours of the rings so far traversed, rose pink, emerald green, orange and gold. The spirit recognises its connection to a spiritual line, the line of all of those who breathe in consciousness of their Divine point, and breathe out the light of blessing. In this way they mirror the action of the Divine breath.

The breath of blessing is the breath of those who celebrate their life, in joyful recognition of their eternal breath. As it breathes in the rose pink light, the spirit understands that the symbol of this ring is an open chest that spills forth an endless supply of wealth. The treasury of the ages is a chest of blessing that is never depleted or diminished. The wealth within this chest wants to be distributed, for its distribution causes it further increase. The more that is taken from it, the more there is to give, for this supply is never exhausted.

THE ARCHETYPE OF THE RING OF BLESSING

As it understands this symbol the spirit finds within itself the archetype of the generous giver, one who distributes a legacy of grace. The spirit that wears the robe of blessing has discovered within itself the largesse of the Divine breath. In this ring they come of age, and their investiture is a sign of their spiritual maturity. The key to this chest of blessing is buried in all of us. The individual whose consciousness reaches this ring has learned to unlock their own inner treasury through the key of their breath.

THE INNERMOST DOME

The other spirits, who have witnessed this investiture, turn with the newly robed spirit in the ring. Their celebration fills the dome with light, and showers of light fall down to the rings below. As they turn the rose pink ring begins to contract. The spirit now finds itself being propelled gently upwards and inwards, into a pale blue ring. It finds itself turning in a sapphire blue ring, the ring of compassionate peace.

THE RAY OF ABUNDANT BLESSING

A rose coloured ray of blessing falls down to earth from a window in the inner dome. This is a ray that encourages generosity of heart and spirit. We feel its influence when a happy marriage is celebrated, when a much longed for child is born, when a cherished career begins. This ray blesses important stepping stones in our lives, and helps to ensure our material and spiritual well being.

The deeper blessing of this ray touches us when we experience sweet states in meditation and prayer; it brings spiritual states of delight and refreshment. It leads us in the right direction, towards the sweetness of grace and away from the bitterness of paths that have no light. It is a ray that connects us to the grace of those who shared this light before, so that we feel their spiritual strength and blessing. It is a light that always brings increase in faith, hope and joy.

THE ANGELS OF BLESSING

The angels of this ray bring the rose pink light of generosity and good will. They are found whenever human life is celebrated and blessed. They are present at weddings, at the birth of children, at gatherings where people come together to wish others well. Their presence spreads happiness, hospitality and good cheer.

Although these angels are attracted to celebratory gatherings, they also visit the isolated and impoverished. They come to the solitary, to those who choose to remember the Divine alone. They bring them a sweet blessing, a blessing of abundant grace. They visit those whose lives are empty and sterile, devoid of laughter and joy. They share the generosity of grace with those who have nothing to give, and nothing to celebrate.

RECEIVING THE RAY OF BLESSING IN THE RIGHT SPIRIT

If you would like to feel a ray of abundant blessing in your life, you can receive it. It is best to ask for this light in a reverent spirit, for this is how the gift of blessing is best received. If you ask for it with greed, in hope of material or spiritual reward, you will block its way. You will be asking in the spirit of greed that always wants more because it fears that there is not enough. If you don't know how to ask in a reverent spirit, before you ask the ray to descend follow these three simple steps:

1. Have a shower, or wash, and put on some clean clothes.
2. Say a short prayer, before you repeat the invocation. It can either be one that you know, or one that you make up. Say it with sincerity.
3. When you ask for the ray to descend, include the following sentence in the invocation :

"May I receive the blessing of this ray with reverence and gratitude."

If you follow these simple steps with sincerity your request will be in the right spirit. You can follow the same procedure before asking for any of the rays, if you feel you need to.

RECEPTION OF THE RAY OF ABUNDANT BLESSING
Follow the instructions for grounding yourself that are found at the end of the book.

Take a few moments to be grateful for your breath. When you are ready say:

"May I receive the grace of the rose pink ray of abundant blessing. May the angels of blessing please be with me."

Then see a ring of rose pink light about a foot above your head, and see a ray descending from this ring to your crown. Let the rose coloured ray enter your crown, and flow down your spine, into the ground beneath you. Then bring the ray back up your spine, and into your heart centre. Let the ray crystallise into a rose pink jewel in your heart.

THE ASSISTANCE OF THE ANGELS OF BLESSING
You may sense the presence of an angel of blessing standing in front of you. If you do, let yourself be supported by this angel, as you receive their blessing. Feel another rose pink ray flowing to you from the ring above. Let a shower of rose scented light

envelop your outer body in its ray.

Whether or not you feel an angels presence, be aware of the sweetness of this rose scented rain of light. Let this shower of light enter the stream of your breath. Breathe in the rose scented light. As you breathe out release the negative thoughts and feelings you have held in your breath. Breathe out the colours of your bitterness, hate and fear. Release those that you have blamed, those whom you could not forgive. Then fill the space they leave behind with a breath of rose scented light.

As you breathe the breath of blessing remember the pink jewel in the heart. See a tiny point of light within it, and focus on this point as you breathe. This point is the spark of your inner light, the spark of your everlasting breath. Breathe in the rose pink rain, and let it feed your inner point. Breathe in celebration of an eternal blessing.

When you have breathed in the rain of grace for long enough, gradually let this shower of sweetness return to the ring above. Let the angel ascend also, if you sensed one. Let the jewel remain in your heart, and as you breathe in gratitude for the blessing of your breath, say:

" *I thank the ray of abundant blessing for the rain of its grace.* "

Make sure you are well grounded before you open your eyes.

THE DEEPER RECEPTION OF THE RAY OF ABUNDANT BLESSING
Once you are familiar with stage one you can go on to receive a deeper dimension of this rays blessing, if you wish.

After sending back the ray of rose coloured light, and its angel, breathe in awareness of the pink jewel in the heart. Then say:

*"May I receive the deeper grace of the rose pink ray of abundant blessing.
May I feel the blessing of its ring."*

As you breathe out let a ring extend from your heart centre to two feet around your body. As you breathe in let this ring contract to the jewel in your heart. Then let the ring extend and stay still. If you like you can repeat the word 'Blessing' as you breathe, feeling the blessing of your ring.

Slowly bring down the ring above your head, to meet and merge with the ring around your body. Let it expand as you bring it down so that it is the same size as the ring that encircles you. Feel the energy of blessing surrounding you. Visualise many little streams of pink light flowing from the ring around you to the jewel in your heart. The little streams of light are like the spokes of a cartwheel, flowing inwards to a central point. The ring around your heart is the outer circumference of this wheel; the rose pink jewel within you is its central stone.

Then slowly let the wheel of blessing turn. As it turns to the right, let the little spokes of the wheel fill the jewel in your heart with light. Feed upon the beauty of heart and spirit of the friends of grace. Feel the strength and illumination of their blessing. Be aware that this ring holds the breath of all of those who lived to bring a blessing to the earth. If you revere a particular saint, prophet or great teacher, feel their blessing flowing to your heart through a wheel of grace.

The blessing of this wheel is the blessing of the friends that you receive with an open heart and a reverent breath. The blessing of the friends is the blessing of our essential grace. It is the grace of an eternal spark that is common to us all. Through a wheel of blessing the light of the friends is released, in order to illumine your heart. The friends of grace need nothing back. They exist to give and share illumination on every level, and the dimensions of time and space do not limit their giving. Receive as much of their light as you need. When you have had enough, contract the wheel to the pink jewel in your heart. Hold this precious stone in your heart as you say:

"I thank the ray of abundant blessing for the blessing of its ring."

Make sure you are grounded and centred before you open your eyes.

SHARING THIS RING WITH ANOTHER PERSON

The healing of this ring is especially for those who feel emotionally and spiritually empty. It heals sterility of heart and spirit, feeding those who have nothing to give and nothing to share. If you know of someone who feels this empty, you can share this blessing with them, if they want it.

People who are recovering from addictions will find the influence of this ray beneficial. It feeds the spirit in a way that many have tried unsuccessfully to do through consuming alcohol or narcotics to excess. The lights of grace feed but cannot harm, and it is impossible to receive too much of them. Your own spiritual development will dictate how much light you can take in.

After having done stage one of the reception, go on to stage two. Then repeat:

"May we feel the deeper grace of the rose pink ray of abundant blessing.
May we feel the blessing of its ring.
May the angels of blessing please be with us."

Feel the rose pink stone in the heart, and extend this to form a ring, four feet around you both. See the ring above you, and then bring this ring down to meet and merge with the ring around you both. Let it expand as it descends so that it is the right size to merge with the ring that encircles you both. Feel spokes of rose pink light radiating from the ring inwards to the jewel in your heart. From your heart send a ray of pink light to the heart of your friend. Feel held by a wheel of blessing that energises your divine spark. When you have both received enough, contract the wheel to the jewel in your heart. Thank the ring for its blessing, and for the blessing of its angels.

SHARING THIS RING IN A GROUP

You can also share the blessing of this ring with a group of people. This ring can be used in a group where people are recovering from a physical or mental illness, which has left them feeling depleted and empty. It can also be used by people who are looking for something to fill an inner vacuum, who are looking for spiritual nourishment. It will be of benefit to any group of people recovering from alcoholism or other addictions.

Let the group stand or sit in a circle. Then as they repeat the above invocation, let each group member visualise a large rose pink ring about a foot above the heads of the entire group. Let each group member receive a ray from the communal ring. Let it enter at their crown, ground them to the earth, and crystalise as a jewel in the heart. From this jewel let them create their own rose pink ring around their heart. Let these individual rings merge into one big ring that surrounds the group. Then slowly bring down the communal ring above everyone's head to meet the ring that encircles the group. Feel it holding the group in a wheel of rose pink light. Let little spokes radiate inwards from the circumference of this great wheel, to connect with every person's heart.

Then let the great wheel of blessing turn. Through the turning of the great wheel, let the light of blessing feed all members of the group. Let everyone receive the blessed communion of the friends as they hold hands in a ring of blessing. Let everyone receive the nourishment of blessing that strengthens and purifies the heart and spirit. Then let the ring contract to the rose jewel within each one, as they give thanks for its blessing.

THE WINDOW OF COMPASSIONATE PEACE

The spirit is carried inwards and upwards by the contraction of the rose pink ring; it now finds itself in a sapphire blue ring, the ring of compassionate peace.

A COMPASSIONATE CONNECTION TO ALL BEING

Turning within the sapphire ring the spirit feels a compassionate connection to all being. It feels the pain of all life in its struggle to evolve and grow. If you have reached a certain level in your own growth, you feel the pain of others, for you suffer with the whole. Within the ring of compassion, the spirit touches again this level of being, and shares the accumulated weight of the suffering of the whole. It feels a sense of connection to every being that is in the dark, every being that has lost its way. It understands that compassion can heal this pain, for compassion is the light in the human heart that leads to understanding. The spirit recognises that the essential nature of compassion is a connection of loving understanding to everything alive.

A COMPASSIONATE TRUST

In its receptive state the spirit knows that embracing this ring involves accepting the trust to care for all life, as all life is supported by this compassionate energy. To accept this trust means being willing to share the light of compassion with any who are lost without it. It also means being willing to share the burdens of those who for a time cannot carry them alone. In accepting to feel deeply and to care, the spirit affirms its connection to the earth. It agrees to share the burdens of its brothers, rather than seek refuge in a higher realm, a realm of rarefied spiritual experience. By choosing to feel on every level, the spirit accepts its own humanity and its place in its present lifetime on earth.

THE SYMBOL OF COMPASSION

As it turns in the sapphire ring, the spirit discovers that the symbol of compassion is a tear. This is the tear that falls as we suffer with another. This tear is a gift, for it holds within it the compassionate love that unifies and heals. As it suffers with its brothers and sisters, experiencing the weight of their pain, the spirit feels the healing power of compassion emanating from this ring.

The spirit now understands how grace is compassionate. It sees that being compassionate means being able to stand under creation and hold it up. Through being compassionate you support the created universe, and bring it peace.

THE ARCHETYPE OF THE RING OF COMPASSION

The spirit held by the sapphire light finds itself losing its individual form, as it merges with the energy of this ring. This merging enables the spirit to fully realise its own compassionate essence. When it returns to itself, its face is transfigured by the light of compassionate grace. Its Christ-like nature is brought to light, as it recognises within itself the archetype of the compassionate Christ. This archetype is dormant in all of us, waiting to be recognised. As the spirit recognises its own compassionate nature, it discovers its Christ-like face.

In the inner dome of grace, the spirit that has recognised its compassionate face now wears a crown of thorns. The thorns are the symbol of the suffering that the spirit shares for love's sake. Through its connection to all life it has chosen to feel the suffering of all, and through such a sharing to help to heal it. Roses grow between the thorns, the symbol of suffering transcended. They stand for the beauty that transforms our suffering, as we see through it to the everlasting reality of grace. Seeing through the crown of thorns, the spirit understands that essential grace is the reality behind all else, including all experience of suffering.

The spirits of others in the dome, who have recognised their compassionate face, share in the experience of the newly crowned spirit. The spirit now turns around gracefully within the ring, and its turning renews the light of the fire below, to which it is connected through a transcendent cord. At this point it finds itself being carried gently upwards and inwards to a ring of indigo blue light, the ring of sacred healing.

THE RAY OF COMPASSIONATE PEACE

The sapphire light of compassionate peace falls down to earth through a window in the inner dome. This ray touches you every time your heart opens to give and receive compassionate love. It is a ray that helps you reach out to another, to give them your support, your love. It helps you to see beyond yourself, to see others as your brothers and sisters. It helps you feel the suffering of others, to share, to care and to heal. It is a ray that humanises your being and ennobles your spirit.

The ray of compassion takes your burdens as it takes your fears, and brings you the blessing of peace. This blessing brings you safety from fear, by bringing you the grace of the Christ. This is the grace of your true self, the part of you that is the Christ. This part of you is never disturbed, it is always calm. This ray, by resonating with your own serene Christ-like self, brings you back to peace, the peace that you forgot in the dark night of your troubled dreams. This blessing wakens you to the truth of who you really are, an awakening that brings peace.

THE ANGELS OF COMPASSION

The angels of this ray bring the sapphire blue light of compassionate understanding. They are found in places where people and animals are cared for with love and kindness. They are found in hospitals where the physically or mentally sick are cared for with compassion. They are also found where the very old and the very young are cared for with loving attention. Any who care lovingly for those who have been hurt or abused, attract the angels of this ray. They are also attracted to places where ill or unwanted animals are cared for with compassion.

The sapphire angels are angels of service, and they stand behind those whose vocation in this world is to serve with love. They give strength of spirit to carers whose compassionate hearts are big enough to support others. These angels are an invisible support; they bring energy, inspiration and healing to those who care for creation.

RECEPTION OF THE RAY OF COMPASSIONATE PEACE

Follow the instructions for grounding yourself that are found at the end of the book.

When you are ready to receive this ray repeat:

"May I receive the grace of the sapphire ray of compassionate peace. May the angels of compassion please be with me."

Let a blue ray descend to you from a sapphire blue ring one foot above your head. Let this ray enter your body at the crown, come down your neck and spine, and go out into the earth beneath you. Bring it back up your spine, to your heart area. Let the ray crystallise into a sapphire jewel in your heart centre. From this gem feel teardrops of blue light filling your heart. Let these tears wash over your whole body, filling your chest, then flowing into your arms and legs. Let the sapphire tears wash away all that you have kept tightly held to your chest, all the pain that you have buried in your heart. Gradually uncover your wounds. The physical wounds and the mental, and the hidden emotional wounds that you have long denied.

THE ASSISTANCE OF THE ANGELS OF COMPASSION
At this point you may become aware of an angel standing in front of you with arms outstretched. Accept the support of this angel, as another ray of sapphire light descends on you from the ring above. This one will envelop your whole outer body in its ray. Supported by an angel of service, and held by the sapphire ray, let yourself receive. As you receive this unconditional support let yourself cry, if you feel like it. Let yourself cry as you release the pain of old wounds kept captive for so long in your brave outer life. As you release your tears, release your pain, as the angel holds you in a beam of sapphire blue. Open yourself to this ray in the knowledge that you can trust it, that it loves you as it heals you.

Allow the sapphire ray and its angel to hold you and heal you, as you release the weight of your suffering, and the responsibility of your caring. Allow yourself to be cared for, and feel this caring flowing from an endless source. Give to this ray all the caring you have given, the years of caring, and the hours. Take from this light all that you need. Take from it the rest, the recuperation, the support and the friendship. Know that it wants you to take it. The compassionate face of our heart opens like a flower to this ray. All of us in our deepest hearts long to live in full recognition of this light, as we find our true Christ-like self.

When you have received enough support release the angel, if you felt one, and let it ascend back up to the ring on the sapphire ray. Let the teardrops of light within you return to the sapphire jewel in your chest. Sit quietly and feel how rested and refreshed you feel. Be aware that this light and its angels are always available to support you. Be aware that they can take and absorb all the negativity that you give them, and that they can transform your pain and fatigue through the energy of their compassionate love.

As you hold the blue stone in your heart, remember to say:

"I thank the ray of compassionate peace for the tears of its grace."

Make sure you are well grounded and centred before you open your eyes.

THE DEEPER RECEPTION OF THE RAY OF COMPASSIONATE PEACE

When you are familiar with the reception of this ray, you can go on to stage two.

After sending back the angel and its ray, continue to feel the sapphire jewel in the heart, filling your body with teardrops of healing blue light. Then say:

"May I feel the deeper grace of the sapphire ray of compassionate peace. May I feel the blessing of its ring."

Bring the teardrops of light flowing through your body back to their source in the sapphire in the heart. Then from this stone let a ring extend, at the level of your heart, two feet all around your body. Focus on the sapphire in the heart, encircled by a ring. As you breathe in contract this ring inwards to the blue jewel in the heart. As you breathe out expand the ring until it surrounds you. Then breathe in the stillness of a sapphire ring, and repeat the word 'Peace'. Feel the peace of a ring of compassionate grace that carries all burdens and calms all fears.

When you are ready, slowly bring down the blue ring above your head to meet and merge with the blue ring around your heart. Let it expand as it descends so that it is the right size to merge with the ring around you. As the rings unite you may feel the touch of an angel of service standing behind you, with hands upon your shoulders.

Then focus on your heart, and find there the sapphire stone of compassionate grace. Visualise many little streams of light flowing from the ring around you to the jewel at your heart. The little streams of light are like the spokes of a cartwheel, flowing inwards to a central point. The ring around your heart is the outer circumference of the wheel; the sapphire in the heart is the central jewel. Let yourself be fed by this wheel of peace. Feel streams of blue energy flowing to your heart from the ring around you. As your heart receives this nourishment, let the sapphire in your heart begin to turn. Feel your jewel of compassionate grace turning within a wheel of peace. Feel the energy of compassionate peace flowing to you, an energy that forgives, mends and calms. Let it change your energy as it brings you its blessing.

When you have received the spiritual nourishment of the ring of compassionate peace, let it contract to the sapphire in the heart, and let this jewel rest within you. Give thanks for this ray of grace as you say:

"I thank the ray of compassionate peace for the blessing of its ring"

Make sure you are grounded and centred before you open your eyes.

SHARING THIS RING WITH ANOTHER PERSON
If you are with someone who is distraught and in need of peace, you can share this ray with them. Remember the invocation, the colour of the ray, and the sapphire in the heart. When you are ready to form the ring, say:

"May we receive the deeper grace of the ray of compassionate peace.
May we feel the blessing of its ring.
May the angels of compassion please be with us."

Extend the jewel in your heart to form a ring four feet around you and the other person. Then slowly bring down the sapphire ring above your head, to meet and merge with the ring around you both. Let it adjust its size as it descends, to fit the circumference of the ring that encircles you. Hold the hands of the friend you are with, and concentrate on the peace of the ring that holds you both. Feel the support of the angels of compassion who hold you both in a sapphire ray of healing light. Let the ring around you both send out little streams of light to the sapphire in your heart. And then from this jewel in your heart, send a ray to the heart of your friend. Feed their heart with the grace of the wheel of peace. This ring brings a peaceful trust; it banishes fear through the grace of pure compassion. This is the grace of the Christ, and all of us can share it, as we share a blessing of peace.

SHARING THIS RING IN A GROUP
You can also use this ring in a gathering, where many people are present. This can be done at times of distress and disturbance, when many people are afraid. It can also be done when many who care for others meet together to seek support. The grace of a ring is amplified in a gathering. All receive the blessing of its peace.

Let the group stand in a circle. Then as they repeat the invocation, let each group member visualise a pale blue ring about a foot above the heads of the entire group. Let each group member receive a ray from the communal ring. Let it enter at the crown, ground them to the earth, and crystalise as a sapphire jewel in the heart. From this jewel let them create their own sapphire blue ring around their heart. Then let these individual rings merge into one big ring that encircles the group.

Then let the group bring down the large ring above them to meet and merge with the ring that surrounds the group. Let this ring send out little spokes of light to the heart of everyone in the group, so that all of you are fed by a great wheel of compassionate peace. Let the little spokes of blue light turn the sapphires in everyone's heart. Receive the grace of this ring, as all of you join hands together sharing a blessing of peace.

THE WINDOW OF SACRED HEALING

The spirit is carried upwards and inwards, into the indigo blue ring of sacred healing. This ring turns from sapphire blue at its outer edge, to indigo and then to purple at its inner edge. As the spirit turns in this ring it is bathed in indigo light, and experiences a deep healing.

THE HEALING OF THE PAST

The energy of the indigo ring is one of sacred healing; the healing that comes from the whole. For only the whole that knows itself can enable the part to understand with clarity its own soul journey. And only the whole can help the part to release itself from worn out patterns of behaviour, which no longer serve its development. The energy of this ring removes from the spirit the negative imprints of previous lifetimes. The spirit receives the powerful light of this ring, which heals and makes whole its spiritual history.

THE SYMBOL OF THE RING OF SACRED HEALING

The spirit that heals its history understands that the symbol of this ring is a golden staff. This staff represents the inner spirit of a person, which cannot be broken or destroyed. True healing comes from recognition of this inner spirit, and complete faith in its perfect wholeness. Recognition of your whole spirit returns you to health on the spiritual, mental, emotional and physical levels.

THE GRACE OF A TRUE HEALING

The spirit that is bathed in the indigo light of this ring loses its boundaries, and experiences the grace of a true healing. It understands with perfect clarity that its journey through lifetimes in form was a journey back to recognition of its healed self. It heals itself as it looks with compassion on all its mistakes, and forgives itself all its past lives of suffering. All the tangled hopes, all the lost opportunities, all the broken dreams and all the unwise choices are forgiven, as it understands that however long its journey, its return is assured. It also forgives itself the past lives of power, the lives where it oppressed others and made them suffer. It understands that at root, however misguided, it was always searching for its own integration, trying to heal its fragmented soul. Now in the indigo ring of sacred healing, it forgives itself for its search, having found the healing integration that it always sought.

THE ARCHETYPE OF THE RING OF HEALING

As it turns in the indigo light the spirit understands the archetype of this ring, the archetype of the sacred healer. The sacred healer is one who has experienced the pain of disintegration, of lack of wholeness, of a divided soul. Through their spiritual and human journey they have returned to health and strength, the strength of spirit that makes them well. The golden staff that they carry represents their spiritual authority, their ability to show others the way to true health of spirit.

The sacred healer can help others to find their own spiritual strength as they help them return to wholeness. Through discovering both the integrity of their soul, and their connection to the wider universe, the sick person can be helped to recover the strength and power of their indestructible spirit.

THE RAY OF SACRED HEALING

The ray of sacred healing is a ray that touches true healers, those who have sworn inwardly to preserve life. As their being reaches this level, the indigo ray anoints them, as they dedicate their lives to the healing of the whole. They are given the spiritual authority to help others on their journey of return to wholeness.

This ray also touches people at moments when they feel the beauty of true reverence. True reverence is an emotion of deep respect for the Divine. The indigo ray touches people when they feel this sacred reverence, whether they find it in the rhythms of nature, or in the ceremonies of a particular spiritual tradition. It helps them feel a sense of connection to the Divine breath that moves the cosmos with order and grace. As we become conscious of the dignity and beauty of the sacred dance of life, we enable the indigo ray to touch our soul and heal us.

THE ANGELS OF HEALING

The angels of this ray bring the indigo light of sacred understanding. They are found where sacred healers work. They stand behind those who are dedicated to the healing of the whole.

They also visit those who are sick, who have no healers to help them. They visit them in dreams or visions, inspiring them with deep spiritual understanding. Through the assistance of these angels the sick person is able to understand more clearly how and why they lost their integrity of soul. Through understanding their scattered state, they can begin to return to health. To heal yourself is to find a path to inner integration and trust. The angels of the indigo ray, being messengers of the whole, can help you see your path to wholeness and inner strength.

RECEPTION OF THE RAY OF SACRED HEALING

If you would like to receive a ray of sacred healing, you can ask for it.

Follow the instructions at the end of the book for grounding and centring yourself.

Then say:

"May I receive the grace of the indigo ray of sacred healing. May the angels of healing please be with me."

Imagine a ring of indigo light one foot above your head. Let a ray descend from this ring, and enter your body at your crown. Let the indigo ray travel down your spine, and out into the earth beneath you. Then let it travel back up your spine to a point level with your navel. Bring the indigo ray forward from here, to rest in the centre of your body. Let the ray crystallise into an indigo jewel.

You may sense the presence of an angel of healing standing in front of you. Let the angel hold you as you receive another ray from the indigo ring, a ray that falls to envelop your outer body in its beam. Let the vibration of this colour calm and soothe you as you breathe in the radiance of this ray. Give to the angel all your broken promises, as you remember all the times that you were less than strong. As you reveal your weakness know that there is no judgement. The rays and their angels will not judge you. They will understand, and they will help you heal.

Turn your attention to the indigo stone within. Let it turn into a golden staff with an indigo jewel at its centre. This staff is about a foot long and its central jewel rests in your centre. Let this staff begin to turn to the right. As it turns let it trace an indigo circle around itself. Feel the security of your centre, as you trace a circle of indigo light around an indigo jewel. Know that the security of your centre is the security of your truth. Breathe deeply into your centre as the staff turns, and feel held in a circle of sacred trust.

After some time, let the golden staff become still. Contract it to the indigo stone at its centre. Let the angel and its ray return to the ring above as you say:

"I thank the ray of healing for the staff of its grace."

Make sure you are grounded and centred before you open your eyes.

THE DEEPER RECEPTION OF THE RAY OF SACRED HEALING
If you want to receive the deeper blessing of this ring, you can. Do stage one and let the staff rest in your centre. Then say:

"May I receive the deeper grace of the indigo ray of sacred healing.
May I feel the blessing of its ring."

Let the staff expand from your centre until it extends two feet in front of your body and two feet behind you. Let it slowly begin to turn, tracing an indigo circle two feet around your body. The centre of the circle is the indigo stone at your centre.

As the indigo ring around you turns repeat the word 'Trust'. The power of a true healing is the power of a sacred trust. A sacred trust is a trust you make with your own truth, with the divine spark within you. As you feel the blessing of an indigo ring trust yourself to heal. Trust that your indestructable spirit is always whole, and no matter how many times you deny it, your inner light can be trusted.

Turn your attention to the ring above your head and slowly bring it down to meet and merge with the indigo ring around your body. Let it expand as it descends so that it is the right size to merge with the ring that surrounds you. As the rings merge, contract the staff to the jewel at its centre. Visualise many little streams of light flowing from the ring around you to the indigo jewel at your centre. The ring around you is the outer circumference of a wheel; the indigo jewel within you is its central jewel. Let yourself be fed by the wheel of sacred healing. Feel streams of indigo energy flowing to your centre from the ring around you.

Let the wheel of sacred healing turn, as it feeds your central stone. As the wheel turns, let the golden staff grow vertically from your central stone. Let the staff grow, so that one end points to the sky, and the other end points down to the earth. As the wheel of healing turns let the golden staff extend. Let it grow downwards into the earth between your legs. And let it extend upwards as far as your crown. As the wheel turns let it strengthen your golden staff. Feel the energy of sacred healing returning you to strength. Know that true strength lies in connection and trust. Feel your connection to the earth below you and the sky above you.

Gradually let the wheel of sacred healing become still. Contract the staff to its central jewel. Contract the wheel around you to this jewel also. Treasure this jewel within as you give thanks, saying:

"I thank the ray of sacred healing for the blessing of its ring."

Ground and centre yourself before you open your eyes.

SHARING THIS RING WITH ANOTHER PERSON
You can share the ring of sacred healing with anyone who is sick, spiritually, mentally, emotionally or physically. It will help if they can have some time to talk with you, both before and after the reception. During this period of talking, encourage them to unburden themselves, to bring to mind past experiences where they lacked integrity, broke promises, deceived others or themselves. It is important that the person listening shows no judgement or criticism, but acts as a truly compassionate presence.

After the reception let the sick person talk again, of how they want to live their life in order to heal themselves. Let them be guided by their inner guidance. Do not attempt to persuade or suggest, just listen. All that matters is that the sick person is able to make a commitment to trust something. Then teach them to do the reception themselves, so that they can do it daily. Encourage them to use it to assist in the healing of their body, mind, heart and spirit. It is important that the sick person understands that a sacred trust is a trust they make with themselves, with their own spirit, not with anyone else. It is their responsibility, and it is their choice to break their trust or keep it.

Do stage one and ask for the angels of healing to be with you both. Let the indigo stone in your centre turn into a golden staff, and then proceed to stage two as you say:

"May we receive the deeper grace of the indigo ray of sacred healing. May we feel the blessing of its ring"

Let the staff extend to four feet around you both. Then let it trace an indigo ring that holds you both in its embrace. Bring down the ring above your head to meet and merge with the ring around you both. Let it expand as it descends, so that it can merge with the ring that encircles you both. Then contract the staff to the stone at your centre, as the wheel of healing feeds your central stone with indigo light. From this stone send a ray of indigo light to your friend. Send it to their central point, at their navel. Let them receive the blessing and benefit of this ring of sacred healing. As the wheel turns, let your indigo stone turn into a vertical golden staff. Let it extend down into the earth beneath you, and up to your crown. As you grow in grounded healing energy send more to your friend. Let your healing increase their healing. When you have had enough contract the staff and the wheel of healing to the indigo jewel at your centre. Give thanks for this ray and the blessing of its ring.

SHARING THIS RING IN A GROUP
The ring of sacred healing can be shared in a group where people come together seeking to heal their mental, emotional and physical ills. It can also be used for groups of people who find that they have no inner strength, who cannot keep promises to themselves or others.

Let the group stand in a circle. Let each group member visualise a large indigo blue ring about one foot above the heads of the entire group. From this communal ring let a ray of indigo light descend to each group member. Let everyone in the group do stage one. Then let them proceed to stage two. Let everyone in the group form a ring around themselves with their staff, and then let these little rings merge into one big ring that encircles the group. Let each individual contract their golden staff to the jewel in their centre. Then let them bring down the ring of healing above the group to meet and merge with the big ring around the group. Let everyone feel the strength of a sacred blessing. Let little spokes of light radiate inwards from the big ring to meet everyone's central jewel. Then let these jewels extend into golden rods that fall vertically into the earth so that everyone is anchored. Then let everyone's golden staff rise to their crown. Let everyone feel a horizontal connection to each other as they feel the great wheel of healing turn. Then let one person in the group say:

" We thank the ray of sacred healing for the blessing of its ring.
We share the sacred trust of our divinity with the earth and sky.
We share the sacred trust of brotherhood with each other.
We heal as we trust, and we trust as we heal."

Eventually let everyone in the group contract their vertical staff and their wheel of blessing to the jewel in their centre. Let each group member treasure their jewel as they repeat:

" We thank the ray of sacred healing for the blessing of its ring."

Let everyone make sure that they are fully centred and grounded, before coming back to everyday consciousness.

REMEMBERING A SACRED TRUST
The golden staff that you visualise in this reception is a symbol of your indestructable spirit. Through the day, feel the strength of this staff of gold that nothing can break. However much you lie, kill, cheat, steal or are blindly irreverent, you cannot break the sacred trust of your spirit. As you remember your golden staff, remember your indestructable spirit, and it's pre-destined journey back to health and wholeness.

WINDOWS IN THE INNERMOST DOME OF GRACE

The Window of Eternity

The Window of Divine Love

The Window of Truth

THE WINDOW OF ETERNITY

The ring of sacred healing contracts, and the spirit finds itself moving upwards into a ring of purple light, that is turning in the centre of the innermost dome. The innermost dome is the highest of the domes of grace, and the atmosphere here is purer and clearer than in the domes below. Sounds here carry an echo, and the light of the purple ring has an echoing call. The spirit breathes in the clear air, and feels the spiritual refreshment of this, the highest dome.

THE BREATH OF ETERNAL TIME

Turning in the ring of eternity the spirit begins to lose itself. As it does so it begins to understand the workings of eternal time. It understands that time is breath, and that the breath of eternal time never starts or ends. An out breath initiates the birth of a chain of universes, and an in breath returns this chain to non-existence. Creation returns to the point that first breathed it forth, the uncreated point of grace. This ever-living point never stops breathing, and its breath brings all things to be.

The spirit understands that a whole chain of universes is born and dies within the space of one cosmic breath. And it understands that this has been going on forever, that there were countless chains before this one. Looking ahead, it understands that this universe will end and then a new one begin again, times without number. It understands that all of this activity happens with orderly grace, and that the ring of eternity is part of this harmonious pattern. The spirit understands that at the centre of an endless cycle of universes flowering and dying and being born again, is the point of grace. This is the central point around which all this activity revolves, the point that gives it order and meaning.

AN ETERNAL BREATH

The spirit sees that the breath of eternal time is greater than anything it could conceive, and that the hours of a cosmic day are longer than anything it could imagine. And yet it also understands that although the breathing of cosmic time is awesome, it can be experienced in a moment. It finds itself experiencing this moment, as it begins to breathe with an eternal breath.

As the spirit breathes with an eternal breath, it begins to inhale the note of this ring. As it inhales it becomes filled with echoing sound. The spirit lost in the sound of the ring begins to understand the call of eternal grace. It realises that the call to grace through the ages is the call of our essence, a call that leads us home.

THE SYMBOL OF ETERNITY

The spirit understands that the symbol of eternity is a ring without beginning or end. This ring makes a calling sound. The spirit that hears this call understands that all begins in grace, and then returns to an end in grace, which then becomes a new beginning. Within the purple ring the spirit hears the call to grace, that cuts through illusion as it brings all being back to grace. The spirit becomes part of an eternal company, those who echo the true call of this ring.

THE CALL TO GRACE

The spirit in the ring now begins to call, and its call echoes the sound of all who called in this ring before. Through sharing their call, the spirit shares in the eternal communion of their spirit. It experiences the communion of this ring, a communion of sound. This communion is a celebration of eternal life. The spirits who merge their call with this ring have understood the tale of eternity, the chain of its breath, and the point of its grace. They know that creation will be born and then return to non-existence on an eternal breath, but that its living essence cannot die. They know that their eternally living essence cannot die either, that it is a point of uncreated grace.

The spirit feels the attraction of this point, and finds itself being pulled inwards, towards the centre of the innermost dome. Here it finds itself in a swiftly turning crimson ring, the ring of divine love.

THE RAY OF ETERNITY

A ray from the window of eternity touches you at moments when the curtain of linear time is blown aside, to reveal the vista of eternity. Through the window of a birth or death this vista can be seen, for at such moments this ray can bring you a glimpse of the eternal pattern behind all life.

This ray brings the light of certainty, a light that calms your fear of death, your anxiety before the unknown. Through the influence of this ray you are helped to see the purpose of your lives and deaths, the learning pattern behind all experience. It helps you to realise that your lifetimes are leading you to a deeper understanding of the reality of love.

THE ANGELS OF ETERNITY

The angels of this ray bring the purple light of spiritual vision and timeless understanding. They are present at a birth or death; they are there to assist each soul making a transition from one state to another. They bring comfort to those who are frightened of change. All of us can benefit from the influence of this light, as it calms our fear of disruption, and helps us to see the beginning in every end.

The angels of the eternal ray also stand behind those whose pioneering work in any field is for the good of humankind. They inspire those who are ahead of their time, for they bring an eternal ray that takes a person beyond the limits of their historical age. This ray brings with it the memory of an eternal call, a call that quickens evolution. This is the inspirational quality of this ray.

RECEPTION OF THE RAY OF ETERNITY

Follow the exercises for grounding the body that are found at the end of the book.

When you are ready say:

> *"May I feel the grace of the purple ray of eternity.*
> *May the angels of eternity please be with me."*

Imagine a ray of purple light descending from a ring one foot above your head. Let this light enter your body at your crown, then let it flow down your spine, and into the earth beneath you. Then bring the purple ray up your spine, to your head.

Let the ray fill your head with purple light. Feel this light behind your brow, your eyes, your cheeks, and your chin. Take this ray to your throat and fill it with light. Then bring this ray down to your chest. Breathe in the purple light; let it fill your heart. Bring this ray down your spine to a point opposite your navel. Fill your abdomen with purple light. Let the ray rest at a point at your centre, behind your navel. Here let it crystallise into an amethyst jewel. Breathe deeply into your abdomen; breathe into this central point in your being.

THE ASSISTANCE OF THE ANGELS OF ETERNITY

You may feel the touch of an angel in front of you. If so receive their blessing as another purple ray falls from the ring above you. Let this ray hold your outer body in its beam, as an angel of eternity holds you. Feel the healing influence of this ray as you surrender your fear with your breath. Let this ray share with you its breath of eternal peace. Through this breath allow yourself to forget yesterday and tomorrow, and become fully present in the moment. Enjoy the freedom of the moment, which is the freedom of an eternal breath. As a purple ray holds you, surrender to the ageless wisdom of this breath.

Turn to the amethyst jewel within. Let this jewel turn into a tiny silver ring. The purple jewel has become a silver ring at the centre of your being. Then let this little ring within you begin to turn. As it turns, listen to its sound. Let yourself hear the sound of this ray's light. As you hear its clear note, let it call you home. This is the call of your own inner being, the call of your own eternal spirit. Listen to your own note, hear your own call. Be aware that everything alive has its own inner ring, its own call of return. All matter is returning in its own time back to the point from which it began. As you learn to hear your own call, you speed your return to spirit, your return to grace.

If you cannot hear your ring calling, do not worry about it. Focus on the visual aspect of the ring. Your call is within you, whether you can hear it or not. As you attune to the rays of grace you will begin to hear it, when you are ready to do so.

When you have listened for long enough, let your inner ring become still. As it does so, it will become silent. Let the ray of grace that envelops your outer body ascend to the ring above your head, taking with it the angel, if you sensed one. Let the silver ring rest in your centre. Thank the ray for its blessing, as you say:

"I thank the purple ray of eternity for the ring of its grace."

Make sure you are fully grounded and centred before you open your eyes.

THE DEEPER RECEPTION OF THE RAY OF ETERNITY

If you wish, you can receive the deeper blessing of this ray. After sending back the ray and its angel, focus on the tiny silver ring held still at your centre. Then say:

"May I receive the deeper grace of the purple ray of eternity.
May I feel the blessing of its ring."

From the little silver ring let another ring expand, a ring that surrounds you. This ring is silver on the inside edge nearer to your body, and purple on the outside edge. Let this ring expand to about two feet around your body. Contract this ring to the tiny ring within, and then let it expand. As you hold the expanded ring still, breathe deeply and repeat the word 'Return'. This is the essence of this ring; it is a ring that calls all being to return to its source.

Then slowly bring down the ring above your head to meet and merge with the purple silver ring around your body. Let it expand as it descends so that it can merge with the ring that encircles you. From the ring around you let spokes of purple light radiate inwards to the silver ring at your centre. The larger ring around you is the outer circumference of a wheel, and the little ring within you is its centre. Through the spokes of the wheel let purple light flow inwards to the centre of your being. Feed upon this light.

As your being is fed by the wheel of eternity, let the little ring within you begin to turn. As it turns, let it call. Hear again the note of its calling as it receives a blessing of eternal peace. Let yourself rest in an eternal wheel as your spirit echoes an eternal call.

The blessing of the wheel of eternity is the blessing of eternal peace. Feel the certainty of eternal peace, the peace that feeds the universe in its harmonious revolution. Be held by this wheel in awareness of an eternal ring that holds you safely. All of our lives and deaths are held in this ring, part of a pattern that is larger than ourselves. All of us are held in this ring with love, as all of our lives are lessons in loving, lessons that help us return to love. As this wheel turns let it feed you with the certainty that the energy that moves the universe loves you. For no matter how insignificant you are, you are still part of an eternal ring, and this ring was created with a breath of love and tenderness. See through your fear of chaos to the harmonious order of an eternal ring, and know that you are part of this order, part of eternity's ring.

When you have heard enough, let the silver ring within you slow down and become silent. Then let the outer wheel contract to the small silver ring at your centre, as you repeat:

"I thank the ray of eternity for the blessing of its ring."

THE DEEPEST RECEPTION OF THE RAY OF ETERNITY

When you are familiar with stage one and two, you can proceed to a further stage if you wish. It is best not to attempt to do so until you are comfortable with both of the earlier stages.

Feel the wheel of eternity that surrounds you feeding your centre with streams of blessing. Then say:

"May I receive the deepest blessing of the purple ray of eternity. May I receive the communion of the ring."

Hear the silver ring in your centre calling, as it is turned by the wheel of eternity. Then let the big wheel begin to call. Let it echo the note of your little ring, so that the sound is amplified. Be aware that this call is your own contribution to an eternal call that echoes through the ages, the call of all being to return. As you listen let yourself be taken by the turning of this eternal wheel. Let yourself be lost in its call.

As you turn with the wheel, allow yourself to lose your limited perception of time and space. Feel the beauty and grandeur of this ring's revolution. As you lose yourself within it, become aware of your insignificance, and the greatness of the universal chain of which the ring of eternity is a tiny part. Become aware of the scale of universal time, as you recognise the eternity of universes before this one, and after. This universe is a tiny ring in an endless chain of universes that has no end. Then with awe and reverence, share in the call of this ring.

Call inwardly with the wheel of eternity, and feel yourself sharing in the call of its ring. Allow this call to refresh and revive your spirit, as you lose yourself within it. Love is the essence of this eternal call. As you hear the call of this ring, allow yourself to be filled with love for your essence, the point that calls you home. Find your own divine point as you turn an eternal wheel. Find your own point in eternal universal love, and let it carry you home with its call.

Be aware that although we live in separate bodies our spiritual essence is the same. Those who heard this call before were all of those who woke up to the blessing of their eternal life. As you wake up and hear this call, understand that you can never die. Your spiritual essence is indestructible. Hear its eternal call, the call to grace. From the first day to the last day of this universal cycle, lovers of the truth have joined, and will join, this circle, inspired by longing for its call. Join with them in the communion of the ring of eternal life. Although we are many, we are one, for we all possess the same essence, the same living point. Lose yourself in the communion of the ring, which is the communion throughout time and space with all of those who share the blessing of eternal life.

When you have received enough let both rings slow down. As they become still, they will become silent. Slowly contract the wheel of eternity to the silver ring at your centre, as you repeat:

"I thank the ray of eternity for the communion of the ring."

Make sure you are well grounded and centred before you open your eyes.

You can remember the blessing of this ring at any time during the day. You can remember it with each breath. As you remember this ring, remember the blessing that runs through time. Feel the blessing that connects time in an eternal ring of grace. And give thanks as you breathe in remembrance of its call.

SHARING THIS RING WITH ANOTHER PERSON
The healing of this ray can help people who are afraid of change. It can help them by bringing them the blessing of eternal peace. If you know of anyone who is facing change and finding it difficult, you can share the blessing of this ray with them. You can also share it with those who are dying, but always ask for their consent. If this is not possible, ask the person inwardly, if they would like to receive this blessing. If you sense any hesitation at all from them then do not include them in the reception. Receive it yourself, and

THE WINDOW OF ETERNITY

then afterwards sit with them, holding their hand. They will receive anything that they need from you.

Times of birth are too busy for the reception of this ray to be practical. But if you or a friend has had a particularly traumatic labour, the mother and baby (and a friend) can do the reception together at a quieter moment some time in the first few days after birth.

First do stage one. Then say:

" *May we receive the deeper blessing of the ray of eternity. May the angels of eternity please be with us.* "

Then go on to visualise a purple ring extending from the silver ring within you to embrace both yourself and the person, or persons (if it is a mother and baby) you are with. Let this ring extend four feet around you both. Then bring down the purple ring above you to meet and merge with the ring that surrounds you. Let it expand as it descends, to fit the ring that encircles you both. Let spokes of purple light flow in from the circumference of this outer ring, to the silver ring at your centre. From your central ring send a stream of purple light to the person, or persons, you are with. Send it first to their centre, and then let it surround them in a ring. This is a ring of security, a ring of eternal peace. The energy of this ring calms fears and anxieties that originate in a restless confusion over why we are here, and where we are going. It helps people to be content to be in the moment they are in.

SHARING THIS RING IN A GROUP

This ring can be shared in a group where people are faced with fears and uncertainties about the future. It can be used in a group for people with terminal illness. It can also be used for people who are bereaved, who are finding it hard to understand why their life has changed through loss. This ring, like all the rings, brings a gentle blessing. It heals through bringing spiritual nourishment, the nourishment of the lights of eternal grace. This spiritual sustenance helps us to grow in illumination, understanding and peace.

After everyone in the group has done stage one of the reception, go on to stage two. Repeat:

"May we receive the deeper blessing of the purple ray of eternity.
May we feel the blessing of its ring.
May the angels of eternity please be with us."

Let everyone's inner ring expand into a purple silver ring that surrounds him or her. Then let the many silver purple rings merge into one big ring surrounding the group. Bring down the large ring that is above the group. Let it meet and merge with the purple silver ring that surrounds everyone in the circle. From this ring let spokes of light radiate inwards to all group members. Let the inner wheel of each person begin to turn. Then let the outer wheel around the group begin to turn. Then let both rings begin to call. As they do so, let everyone feel the grace of an eternal blessing. This is the blessing that banishes our fear of the unknown. Let everyone's spirit receive the call of this ring, the call that awakens us from fear. When everyone has received enough, let the ring around the group and the rings inside each member slow down, and become silent. Let each person in the group contract the big wheel to the tiny ring in their centre, remembering as they do so that they hold a ring of eternal life within their own being. Remember to say thank you for the ray of eternal grace, and the blessing of its ring.

THE WINDOW OF DIVINE LOVE

Carried by the contraction of the purple ring of eternity, the spirit finds itself moving into a swiftly turning crimson ring, the ring of divine love. This ring turns rapidly in the centre of the innermost dome.

COMING HOME TO DIVINE LOVE

The light of this ring is loving, and the spirit is held in its warm embrace; returning to it feels like coming home. Divine love is the energy that attracts us back to our essence. The attraction that pulls the spirit upwards through the domes is the attraction of grace itself. Grace calls its manifestations to return, and it does so through the attractive power of divine love.

As it loses its form in this ring, the spirit begins to taste the intoxicating beauty of divine love. The overpowering beauty of love renders the spirit incapable of remembering or caring about anything else; it is lost in love, and forgets about its journey and its destination. The truth is more beautiful than anything we could conceive. In this ring the spirit feels this beauty and falls deeply in love with it. It knows that it wants nothing else but to draw nearer to the truth, to witness it.

When the spirit returns to itself it is changed by this experience. It realises that it always wanted this love, that this was the source of all its efforts, all its longing. It realises that for love of the truth it would undergo any experience, however painful.

THE SYMBOL OF THIS RING

In the swiftly turning crimson ring the spirit finds that everything has changed, the way it used to see, the way it used to think, and the way it used to fear. The spirit understands that love is a revolution, and this turning is one that leads it to grace. To turn to love is to leave behind desire for anything else. The spirit is so attracted that it cannot hold back, and offers itself to love with total dedication. Through this dedication the spirit realises the archetype of the true lover, one who gives all for love. As it turns the spirit understands that the symbol of this ring is a crimson rose. The rose is the symbol of lovers who no longer fear death, for they know that love is everlasting.

REVIEWING PAST LIVES

The spirit now sees its own history in a different light. It sees how through its lifetime (or previous lifetimes) on earth, its love has been tested. The individual whose spirit reaches this ring has experienced suffering and pain during a physical incarnation, and seen through this experience. They have recognised the reality of love, that this is what we are here to discover, to understand, and to share. They have learned to love their enemies, for their vision has become fully unified.

Whatever it has suffered on earth, in this ring the spirit understands the true lesson behind these events. It understands how it learned love's lesson, inspired by the beauty of the truth. And it remembers the lesson of forgiveness, the lesson that leads it back to grace.

BECOMING A WITNESS OF DIVINE LOVE

Becoming a witness of divine love means seeing through all illusion, to the truth behind it. One who has become a witness has seen through the illusion of everything but love. Love is their truth. They know that the manifest universe begins and ends in love, and that love itself does not begin or end, it always is. Therefore they have nothing to fear. Their perception is so unified that they do not see anything that happens to them as happening outside the Divine plan.

The witnesses have seen the end, and know that the dance of grace is their destination. They understand that the truest lovers are those who see through all but love, and who do not believe in the permanence of anything except love and grace, whatever their personal fate in the world.

A DOORWAY FOR THE ENERGY OF GRACE

The spirit understands that when you cease to resist wrath, and begin to transform it, you bring a healing. The witness is a doorway for the energy of mercy and grace to come to earth. They are a spiritual poultice for the rest of humanity, drawing out the fear, and giving back the unifying energy of grace.

THE ORDER OF THE ROSE

The reality of the witness is the unifying reality of grace that never dies. As the spirit accepts this reality as its own, the window of grace above them opens. The window of grace is a round window at the top of the innermost dome. Through the open window a rain of crimson roses falls down into the ring. In this way the spirit receives the Order of the Rose, the order of the witnesses of grace. It is accepted and acknowledged as a spirit that has found its way home, through the veil of illusion, through suffering and persecution, back to love.

THE WITNESSES UPHOLD THE UNIVERSE

One who reaches this level in the domes of grace helps to preserve the spiritual balance of the universe, just as the friends do at the stage below. Without their unifying, stabilising and healing influence the spiritual order of the universe would collapse and fall into chaos before its appointed time. Through the proof of their faithful witness they affirm the reality of universal love and grace, and like a pillar uphold the created universe.

THE JOURNEY OF THE MOST ATTRACTED

The spirit is only attracted to this ring if it has proved itself a true lover during an incarnation on earth. Most of the spirits that journey through the domes find their resting place in one of the rings in the inner or outer dome. This will be the ring to which they are attuned, the one that resonates most closely with their own spiritual note. The spirits that journey into the innermost dome are the most attracted. They have been captivated by the beauty of the truth, and have proved the sincerity of their love.

THE PATH OF LOVERS

It is impossible for the spirit to journey this far within the domes if it has not seen through the illusion of fear. Only lovers are so attracted to the truth, that they bear witness to their love through every circumstance, including persecution and death. The path of a friend is lined with gold and precious stones. The crimson path of a lover is for those who have nothing but love. It is for those who give away everything for love, for those who see through all else. It is a path for the few who earn a rose.

THE CONTRACTION OF THE CRIMSON RING

At this point the crimson ring begins to turn even more quickly and starts to contract, coming closer to the centre of the innermost dome. The spirit is consumed with love for its essence, the original point that calls it home. It loves the centre of its essence, and this centre itself is attracting its lover to return. Understanding that the centre of its essence can never die, and that this centre is a point of unified grace, the spirit finds the ring around it rising and contracting to a sphere. As it contracts this ring changes colour from crimson to white. Carried by this contraction the spirit finds itself at the top of the innermost dome in a ball of crystal clear white light.

THE RAY OF DIVINE LOVE

A crimson ray from the window of divine love falls to earth from a window in the innermost dome. Few people feel the full intensity of this ray, but most of us have felt it in a diluted form. This ray touches us when we feel a strong attraction to a person, a place, an endeavour, a creative project, or an idea. It is a ray that pulls separate things together, the force of attraction that leads to union. Some of us have felt the influence of this ray, when we have fallen in love with another human being. We are attracted through the pull of human love, we feel the need to be with the other, to be together, not separate from them.

The way this ray affects the spirit is to fill the individual with a sense of urgent longing that cannot be fulfiled through anything in the material realm. This beam attracts you back to itself, back to your origin in love. It is the pull of divine attraction that can turn a settled life upside down. If you feel the attractive force of this light you will begin a spiritual path in earnest; you will not be able to resist its pull. From this light you will receive a measure of divine love that will propel you home the shortest way.

THE ANGELS OF THE RAY OF LOVE

The angels of this ray bring the crimson light of true love and loving understanding. They are found whenever two people fall in love with the truth in each other. They bless the union of heart and spirit that grows between true lovers. They are also found where the Divine is loved with sincere intensity outside a personal relationship. They visit those who exist for God alone.

The angels of the crimson ray also visit the lovesick and the lonely. The help to mend broken hearts, and heal the bitterness of a broken trust. These angels are found where two people meet to reconcile and forgive. They help people to love again, those who fear to love because of previous pain. They help them to find a deeper capacity to love, a depth of forgiveness and trust found in a love that is unconditional.

RECEPTION OF THE RAY OF DIVINE LOVE
Follow the instructions for grounding and centring yourself that are found at the end of the book.

When you are ready say:

"May I receive the grace of the crimson ray, the ray of divine love. May the angels of love please be with me."

See a crimson ring about a foot above you, turning slowly, and see a crimson ray falling from this ring, onto the crown of your head. Let this ray flow down your head, neck and spine, into the earth beneath you. Then bring the crimson ray back up to your heart. As it fills your heart feel the welcome of this light, feel its love enveloping you and filling you with warmth. Let it crystallise into a ruby jewel in your heart centre. Then let crimson light fill your body.

THE ASSISTANCE OF THE ANGELS OF LOVE
You may sense the presence of a crimson angel standing in front of you. Let the angel hold you as you feel another ray descending from the ring above, a ray that envelops your outer body. Offer to this ray all that you have ever loved. Maybe you loved a person, who is no longer there. Maybe you loved a child who has grown and gone. Maybe you followed faithfully a way of life that now leaves you feeling disillusioned. Whatever you have held in your heart with love, share it with the crimson ray. Share the hidden story of the heart.

If there is any bitterness in your memory, let the crimson light ease your pain. This ray loves you unconditionally, whatever you have done; however you have behaved. It knows that you fear being unloved, and this is why your power to love is weak. It knows that you fear to be hurt, and this is why you close your heart. Under the influence of its ray, let your heart open, in the knowledge that this light will not hurt you. Feel the love of this ray accepting every part of you.

As you receive its light let the ruby jewel turn into a crimson rose in your heart. As you find this rose, let your heart open even further, and feel how it could be to love unconditionally. Feel how it could be to understand the fear behind another's unloving behaviour, to not take it personally, because you know that you are always loved. To give back love, instead of hate and anger, when you are hurt.

When you are ready, let this ray ascend to the ring with its angel. Treasure the rose in your heart as you say:

"I thank the ray of divine love for the rose of its grace."

Make sure you are well grounded and centred before you open your eyes.

THE DEEPER RECEPTION OF THE RAY OF DIVINE LOVE
The deeper reception of this ray has two dimensions. The first dimension feeds the heart, and is suitable for all. To receive it, feel the rose in your heart filling you with crimson light. Then say:

"May I receive the deeper grace of the crimson ray of divine love. May I feel the blessing of its ring."

From the rose in your heart expand a ring outwards about two feet from your body. Contract this crimson ring to the rose in your heart, and then expand it to form a ring around you. Feel this crimson ring around you, as you repeat the word 'Love'. Feel the loving energy of the ring surrounding you. Then slowly bring down the crimson ring above you to meet and merge with the crimson ring around you. Let it expand as it descends so that it can merge with the ring that encircles you. As the rings meet feel the blessing of divine love in a ring around you. Let little spokes of crimson light radiate inwards from this ring to meet the rose in your heart. The outer ring is the circumference of a wheel; the rose in your heart is its centre. Then slowly let the wheel of divine love begin to turn. As it turns let it feed the rose of the heart. Let it feed it with the spiritual strength and purity of all of those who lived for love before. Let yourself receive their blessing, the blessing of the rose. Feel this loving energy flooding your heart with warmth.

Receive this nourishment for as long as you need it. When you are ready, contract this ring to the rose in your heart, as you say:

"I thank the ray of divine love for the blessing of its ring."

Make sure you are well grounded and centred before you open your eyes.

THE DEEPEST RECEPTION OF THE RAY OF DIVINE LOVE
There is a deeper dimension to this ring that you can receive; it is best to ask for it in a spirit of humility and gratitude. This is a spirit that recognises your debt to the witnesses of grace, whose blessing illumines this ring. If you are able to feel this humility and gratitude, then you are ready to receive this ring's deepest blessing.

Continue to receive the nourishment of the wheel of divine love as it feeds the rose in your heart. Then say:

"May I receive the deepest blessing of the crimson ray of divine love.
May I receive the communion of the rose."

Focus on the rose in your heart that is nourished by the wheel of divine love. Feel a crimson rain falling on you, filling the area inside the wheel. As the rain falls, feel the wheel around you beginning to turn, and as it turns let it take the rose of your heart with it. Let the outer ring of the wheel turn its central point. Feel the grace of all of those who send you this rain, that you might feel the deepest blessing of this ring. As the wheel turns repeat the phrase: 'Nothing but love'. Nothing but love is the secret of this ring's revolution, the secret of all of those who bring the crimson rain of grace. Allow yourself to be taken by the turning of this wheel, as you lose yourself in love, as others did before.

As you lose your form, find the certainty of your essence. Your essence does not want you to be anything but loving, for when you are, you are true. Let the ring take you from yourself, to find yourself in love. Love is the truth in you that will not pass away. Lose all for love, for you are in truth nothing but love. Feel the secret of this ring's revolution as you turn to love.

As you find that love is all that you are, you will feel the spiritual influence of those who lost all for love before. Their essence exists in this ring. As you lose yourself and partake of this ring's essence, you share with them the communion of the rose. This is the communion through time and space, with those who gave all for love. This ring contains the light of the souls that healed our history, whose blood fell from the cup of their bodies that we might know that the truth is love. Feel their healing grace now, as the crimson rain falls in the turning ring. They cannot share the light of their communion with you until you are poor, having lost everything for love. Then they can share with you their communion, the communion of lovers of truth. Having lost everything for love, they share with you the everlasting blessing of the rose.

When you have drunk your fill of their grace, the crimson wheel will begin to turn more slowly. Let it stand still, and then contract this wheel to the rose in your heart, as you say:

"I thank the ray of divine love for the communion of the rose."

Let the energy you have shared in this ring change you. Let the beauty of this communion humble you, as you learn to share its blessing.

SHARING THIS RING WITH ANOTHER PERSON

The energy of this ray can help to heal those who have closed their hearts, afraid to love and trust. It can help them to open up and receive love again. You can help another to feel the healing grace of this ray. If you are sure they want it, say:

"May we receive the grace of the crimson ray of divine love.
May we feel the blessing of its ring.
May the angels of love please be with us."

Let the ray descend on you, from a crimson ring above, and form a ruby in your heart. Let this ruby turn into a crimson rose. Let another ray descend and hold both your outer bodies in its ray. Feel the embrace of the angels of love, as your hearts begin to heal. Then let the rose in your heart extend a ring that holds both of you in its embrace. From this ring let spokes of light connect to your heart, and then send this crimson light to the heart of your friend. When you have both received the nourishment of divine love, contract this wheel to the rose in your heart. Remember to thank the ring, and its angels for their blessing.

SHARING THIS RING IN A GROUP

The reception of this ray can be practiced in a group, but not in its deepest dimension. The healing light of this ring is useful for groups of people who find it hard to trust. It can help people who fear to open their hearts to give and receive love. It can be used in groups for adults who have been physically or sexually abused, who because of previous damage find it hard sustain loving relationships. It can also be used where people are trying to rebuild their lives after broken relationships, where faith and trust have been shattered. It is a ring that helps people to love and forgive both others and themselves. It gives them the courage to love.

Let everyone in the group visualise a crimson ring about one foot above the group, as they stand in a circle. Then let everyone in the group say the invocation, feel the ray and form a ruby in their hearts. Let the ruby transform into a rose, and then extend this rose to become a crimson ring round each person. Let each individual ring merge into one large ring of grace, enveloping the group. Bring down the ring above everyone's head to meet and merge with the ring that encircles the company. Then let everyone receive a spoke of crimson light, flowing to their hearts, from the circumference of the great wheel. Let every member feel the healing grace of the wheel of divine love that brings courage, love and trust.

As you contract the ring to the rose in each one's heart, remember to give thanks for the ring and its angels.

THE WINDOW OF TRUTH

THE VIEW FROM THE TOP OF THE UPPERMOST DOME

The spirit now finds itself in a ball of clear white light that is suspended like a diamond at the top of the uppermost, innermost dome. Looking down from this position the spirit can see the different coloured rings fanning out through the domes below. Directly beneath it is the ring of divine love, a small swiftly turning crimson ring. Further down and spreading out from the crimson ring it sees the purple ring of eternity. This ring is encircled by the indigo ring of sacred healing. The sapphire blue ring of compassionate peace surrounds the indigo ring. Further down and further out still the spirit sees the rose pink ring of abundant blessing. This is encircled by the emerald green ring of life, the widest of the rings in the domes. Inside the green ring the spirit can see the yellow gold ring of illumination. Below this, the orange ring of transcendence turns within the golden ring. Rising through the middle of all the rings is a thin column of flame, a burning cord that connects the spirit to the fire of friendship. The spirit can see the red flames of this fire far below, from its vantage point at the top of the innermost dome.

The spirit sees that the three tiers of the domes below are slowly turning; the outer dome and the innermost dome turn in one direction, the inner dome in another. The window arches that radiate the rays of grace are also moving, carried by the stately revolution of the domes. Rays from each ring pour out of the windows in swirling circles of coloured light.

HEAVEN IS WITHIN YOU

Seen from above, the turning rings, the falling rays, and the slowly revolving domes form a kaleidoscopic pattern of great beauty. Coupled with this sight is the sound that issues through the domes, a synthesis of the notes of each ring that blend together in perfect harmony. The spirit breathes in the beauty of the scene below. It knows that this is a realm of grace, where light and sound and colour mingle in perfect harmony. But it also knows with deep understanding that heaven is in the feelings it has experienced on its way. It is in the love, the joy, the generosity, the compassion, the healing and the wonder that the spirit has felt on its journey through the domes of grace.

The spirit knows that heaven is a state of being, and that it does not have to be here, in the domes, to experience this state, for it can find it anywhere. The domes have been a mirror, showing the spirit what it always held within but did not see. In the middle of the innermost, uppermost dome, in the centre of a white sphere, the spirit looks in the mirror and recognises its true self.

THE POINT THAT HOLDS ALL DIMENSIONS

The sphere that holds the spirit is still. Within this stillness the spirit understands that all the rings in the domes through which it passed originate from the place in which it now rests, in a ball of clear white light. The rings manifest different aspects of the energy of creative unity, different attributes, colours, sounds and vibrations. At the centre of this sphere is a point, the point of unity, the point from which all the rings expand, and to which they will return at the end of a universal cycle.

THE DIMENSIONS OF TIME AND SPACE

The spirit understands that the dimension of time springs from this point, time being cyclical, not linear. Thus, each created universal cycle starts and ends at this point. The time that this cycle takes is like the loop of a spiral that begins and ends at the same point. Standing in the centre of its own time, the spirit understands how the point of truth liberates one's vision. It enables one to see through time, rather than be held captive by it, as one is when time is viewed in linear terms.

The spirit understands how this point is also the first point of the spiral of space as a dimension. It is the point from which all spatial relationships spring, containing within it the unfolding of space. All matter originates from this point, for it is the origin of the rings which form the spiritual blueprint for the denser worlds below. The concept of distance, of something being near or far is understood to have a conscious dimension, as the physical distance of phenomena from their source is also their spiritual distance. The forms of the celestial world are closer to their origin than a rock or a stone, because they are more conscious of it. The cycle of space is thus seen to be one in which the physical universe unfolds in a spiral away from its starting point, and then returns as it becomes more spiritually conscious, back to meet the original point of its creation.

The cycles of time and space are understood to be simultaneous. This means that they begin at the same point, and return at the same time to the same point. This is because the end of a particular physical universe is the end of both its created time and space. The spirit understands through its clarified vision that this point of truth is the beginning and end of all created dimensions.

THE BREATH OF TRUTH

As the spirit understands that this point is the origin and the destination of all created dimensions, it begins to breathe with the breath of truth. This is the breath that issues from the still point where creation begins and ends. As it breathes with this breath the illumined spirit remains motionless. It knows that it does not have to travel any further, that it has reached its destination, and recovered its own point. It feels the peace of the truth, the peace of true knowledge that dispels all doubt. That which the spirit knows now, beyond all doubt, is the point where it started from, which is also the point of its return.

THE INFINITE DIMENSIONS OF THIS POINT

Becoming this point the spirit affirms its own truth. It understands that the point of truth is love, but its understanding goes deeper, for the spirit also realises the infinite dimensions of this point. All directions and dimensions lead it to this same point, so that it is taken out of this time and this universe, into an infinite dimension. In other words, in any universe, in any cycle before and after this cycle of time, and before and after this cycle of space, it still has nowhere to go but this point of truth. It understands that the cycles that spring from this point will never end. Although one universe will end, another will always begin, as the Divine lets out its next breath. The breath of truth knows that the Divine can never die, and that therefore its manifestation through its breath can also never end. In the certainty of an infinite breath, the spirit realises its true point.

THE SIMPLICITY OF TRUTH

The spirit breathing in the white light understands the simplicity of the spiritual path that is a return to a starting point, the point of truth, which is love. It understands that all its attempts to mystify and complicate this journey came from its lack of understanding, and its lack of vision. It sees that many on the higher stages of the path lose their way because they lose their simplicity. Instead of seeing clearly, with certainty, they begin to see everything in relation to themselves, and view their own spiritual attainment as proof that they have understood the path.

The spirit sees that it has often done the same, that its vision has not always been clear. At the top of the highest dome the spirit has lost its robe and crown. In its nakedness it understands how pure and simple is the truth, and how pure and simple is its love for it. It sees that the path of return to grace is simple.

THE VERTICAL AND HORIZONTAL PATH TO TRUTH

Understanding the simplicity of the spiritual path, the spirit also sees with clear vision, how humanity has approached this path up till now. It sees that over the past age humanity has viewed the spiritual path from two different perspectives. Some have seen a path to the Divine as a ladder, beginning at faith and rising gradually through various stages, to ascend to the grace of union with the Truth. A relationship with the Divine is the main focus of the vertical path. Others have viewed the spiritual path from a more horizontal perspective, believing that understanding of Truth is attained through an expansive experience of Unity, in which one's being spreads out to embrace the universe. Identification with the Divine through the experience of unity is seen as the key element of this path.

A THREE-DIMENSIONAL PATH TO TRUTH

The spirit understands that both the vertical and horizontal paths lead to truth, in different ways. It sees that the point of any spiritual path is most perfectly realised when the vertical and horizontal paths are combined, so that one's path becomes three-dimensional. The last stage of the journey, which unites the horizontal and vertical dimension, terminates in the centre point of a perfectly rounded sphere, the ball of light in which the spirit now turns. The spirit sees with clarity that the perfect expression of truth is always perfectly simple, round and whole.

THE SYMBOL OF TRUTH

The spirit now understands that the symbol of truth is a point, a point that contains all dimensions within itself. The wine of truth that intoxicates all being is the pure realisation of this point. The spirit at the centre of the innermost dome has no need to travel further, for the aim of its journey has been fulfiled. It has found the point of truth within itself.

THE WINDOW OF GRACE

In the centre of the innermost dome, the spirit looks up, at the round window in the roof above. The window of grace is a turning mosaic of jewelled light. This window resembles the window of friendship, having the same rose pattern, but containing more precious stones. The spirit sees emeralds, pale and dark sapphires, pale and dark rubies, amethysts and diamonds, in a setting of gold. This rose window is turning, revolving slowly, and as it does so coloured rays fall from it down to the rings below. These coloured rays interweave with the lights of the different coloured rings that fill the descending domes. As it looks up the window opens, and the pure spirit looks up through the window of grace.

THE RAY OF TRUTH

A clear ray from the point of truth falls down to earth from the innermost dome. This ray touches us at moments of clarity, when we feel the simplicity and tranquillity of the truth. It is a ray that aligns our being with truth, so that we feel illumined and calm. This ray brings us lasting security, it comes to us when we have nothing left to fight for, and nowhere left to go. It helps us rest in our centre, in the peace of the truth.

This ray also reaches us in those brief moments in our lives when we are inspired to talk or act with courage, honesty and heroism. The resonance of the truth rings through us at such moments, so that what we say or do feels right, and other people feel the pure influence of truth.

THE ANGELS OF TRUTH

The angels of the white ray bring the light of truth and lucid understanding. They stand behind anyone who speaks up for truth. They support those who stand alone against the forces of tyranny; those who are unjustly imprisoned, persecuted, and mistreated. To them they bring the support of the truth, in a ray that brings true vision.

The angels of this ray also touch those who need the healing grace of the truth. They visit those who are tangled up in webs of sadness, illusion and fear. To those whose lives have become confused and fraught, they bring the simple blessing of the pure white ray. They also visit those who have lost their way through the misguided influence of others. They bring the blessing of a ray that restores clarity and direction.

RECEPTION OF THE RAY OF TRUTH

If you would like to feel the influence of this ray, you can do so. Follow the exercises at the end of the book for relaxing and grounding the body.

Then say:

> *"May I receive the grace of the pure white ray of truth.*
> *May the angels of truth please be with me."*

See a clear diamond above your head. Visualise a ray of white light descending from this diamond and entering your body at your crown. Receive the white light; let it flow down the back of your head, down your neck, down your spine, and into the earth beneath you. Then bring the white ray up your spine to your heart centre. Let the white ray crystallise into a diamond in your heart. Breathe into this diamond and let it illumine your heart. Feel the calm, still beauty of this jewel of truth.

THE ASSISTANCE OF THE ANGELS OF TRUTH

In front of you, you may sense the presence of a pure white angel. As you receive their support feel another ray falling from the diamond above you, to envelop your outer body in its beam. As it falls on you breathe in the blessing of the truth. This is a blessing that cures us of deceit. Lose your layers of dissimulation and feel the naked innocence of your true self. In truth you have nothing to hide. When you have breathed in the light of this ray for long enough, let it return to the diamond above your head, with the angel if you sensed one.

Turn to the diamond in your heart and in its centre see a pure spark of white light. Form a chalice, a silver grail, around the diamond in your heart. From the spark at the centre of the diamond let streams of light issue forth, overflowing the chalice within. Through remembrance of your true point, bring forth the wine of truth. Let light from the grail fill your body with radiance, the pure radiance of truth. Know that this chalice always overflows; it cannot run dry, for the truth is always alive.

When you have received enough of the white light, let the grail contract to the diamond at its centre. Keep this diamond in your heart, as you say:

" *I thank the ray of truth for the grail of its grace.*"

Make sure you are grounded and centred before you open your eyes.

THE DEEPER RECEPTION OF THE RAY OF TRUTH
If you want to receive the deeper blessing of this ray, you can. As this is a fairly long meditation, you may want someone else to read it aloud as you do it, for the first few times. Or you may want to record it on a cassette, and play the tape as you receive the ray.

After stage one, continue to focus on the silver chalice in the heart, overflowing with light. Then say:

"May I receive the deeper blessing of the white ray of truth.
May I feel the blessing of its ring."

Focus on the chalice in the heart, and the diamond within it that brings forth light. Then from the jewel in the grail extend a ring two feet around your body. Contract the ring to the jewel in the grail, and then expand it to surround you. Let it become still, as you breathe in its radiance. Repeat the word 'Truth', the essence of the white ring's light.

Then turn your attention to the diamond above your head. Bring this jewel down to your crown, on a ray of white light. Let the diamond enter your head and bring it down your neck and spine, to your heart. Let the diamond from above fall into the chalice in your heart, to meet and merge with the diamond already there.

Now from the diamond in the silver chalice let little spokes of light extend to meet the ring around you. The diamond in the grail within you is the centre of a wheel; the ring around you is its outer circumference. Let the overflowing light from the grail spill out and fill all the little spokes of light radiating out to the edge of the wheel. Let the wheel of truth around you begin to turn, fed by the light of a point within.

As the wheel turns let it change colour. Let it turn from white to crimson. As it does so, realise that the point of truth has always loved you. Feel your own love for your innermost point, the jewel of your own truth. As you feel the energy of the crimson ring, feel the energy of love that turns this ring.

Then let the crimson ring turn purple. As it turns purple remember that the point of truth within the grail outlives both time and space. Feel the wonder of an eternal blessing, the awe-inspiring beauty of an eternal call. As the purple ring turns, let it change to a deep indigo blue.

Held in the indigo ring feel the strength of the truth, the strength of your indestructible spirit. Remember the golden staff of a sacred trust that you cannot break.

Let the indigo ring turn a pale sapphire blue. Feel how the truth supports all life in its struggle to evolve. Feel the compassion of the truth, a compassion that understands without judgement, which suffers with us and shares our tears, so that we may heal and grow.

Let the sapphire ring turn a delicate rose pink. As you turn the rose ring, feel the sweet blessing of a treasury of grace. Feel the generosity of the truth that wants you to receive, that wants to shower you with sweetness. Feel the bounty of true abundance, a giving that never ends.

Let the rose pink ring turn emerald green. Feel the living bless-ing of the truth, a fountain that never runs dry. Feel how life and hope will always overflow from the grail in your heart, for this is the cup of everlasting life.

WINDOWS IN THE INNERMOST DOME OF GRACE

Let the green ring turn to gold. As it turns, feel the illumination of the truth that lit the ages past. Rest in the light and warmth of a true candle, the flame that brings hope as it leads all travellers home.

Let the gold ring turn orange. Feel the transcendent power of the truth, a pillar that connects all creation. Feel the joy of a transcendent blessing, the blessing that enables all of us to gracefully evolve.

Let the wheel turn white as it slows down and becomes still. Rest in the white wheel of truth that contains all the coloured rings within it. Understand that you contain the rings of grace in your own being, for you contain their point of origin. Within this point, the love, the eternity, the trust, the compassion, the generosity, the life, the light and the transcendence of the truth are found. All of these attributes of grace can overflow from you, as you remember their original point. The point that holds all dimensions rests in your heart. You are a perfect mirror of the universe, a tiny miniature of creation, as is all created form.

Let the wheel of truth contract to the chalice in your heart. Then let the grail contract to the diamond point at its centre. Then say:

"I thank the ray of truth for the blessing of its ring."

Make sure you are grounded and centred before you open your eyes.

Make a commitment to remember the truth every day. Make a commitment to remember your true point, and its turning rings of grace. In this way you make a commitment to remember your own divinity and its attributes. All of us can find our true point and return to grace, as we celebrate the rings of grace within ourselves.

THE DEEPEST RECEPTION OF THE RAY OF TRUTH
When you are familiar with stage one and two, you can go on to stage three if you wish.

After having turned the wheel of truth, and experienced the blessing of its rings, let the wheel turn white again. Then repeat:

"May I receive the deepest blessing of the white ray of truth.
May I receive the communion of the grail."

Slowly bring the turning wheel to a standstill. Let light from the diamond in the grail flow outwards in little streams to fill the circumference of the wheel. Then begin to move the wheel in a different way. Let the white wheel become a hoop, which stays with its sides held still, but moves front and back. Let the front of the hoop tip so that it passes under your feet, while the back passes over your head. The wheel now no longer turns around you horizontally; it encircles you in an orbit, creating a bubble of white light around you. As the wheel of truth encircles you, lose yourself in your own radiance. As it turns, find yourself surrounded by a ball of white light.

The overflowing energy of the point within the grail is the energy of love. This is the light that fills the wheel and causes it to turn in new directions. As the wheel turns around you creating a ball of light, share in the communion of the grail. Lose yourself within a ball of light, as you lose this time and this place. Lose track of all cycles of time and space, and know that this point remains. The communion of this point intoxicates the universe. The whole universe is drunk with the wonder and glory of the turning of its own creative point. Everything living is celebrating this point in its own way, it always has and it always will. As you celebrate the infinite dimensions of this point, share in the morning cup of the lovers of the truth. This is they cup they drink from the beginning of one created cycle to its end. Share in the communion of the timeless lovers of truth whose circle embraces the beginning and the end of every universal cycle, and then begins again.

Let the turning white ball of light gradually slow down. As it slows down let the wheel of truth come to rest in its former horizontal position, in front of your heart. Then contract the wheel to the grail in your heart, and contract the grail to the diamond in its centre. Let the diamond in your heart be still. It belongs in your heart, for this is the resting-place of your own truth, the point that you make real. Rest in remembrance of this point as you repeat:

"I thank the ray of truth for the communion of the grail."

Make sure you are grounded and centred before you open your eyes.

SHARING THIS RING WITH ANOTHER PERSON

If you are with someone who is lost in illusion you can share the blessing of this ray with them, a ray which brings clarity and direction. The following meditation can help people to find their own centre, an inner source of light and healing.

Do the first part of the reception, using the following invocation:

" May we receive the grace of the white ray of truth.
May the angels of truth please be with us."

Bring the diamond ray down to rest in your heart, and let a white ray envelop both of your outer bodies in its beam. You may feel the presence of white angels, holding you both tenderly. Let the diamond in your heart turn into a silver chalice, and then repeat:

"May we receive the deeper blessing of the pure white ray of truth.
May we receive the blessing of its ring.
May the angels of truth please be with us."

Bring down the diamond from above your head on a white ray, and let it merge with the jewel in the grail. Let the chalice in your heart overflow with light, forming a wheel around you both. Let the grail in your heart feed the little spokes of light, as they turn the white ring. From your heart send a stream of overflowing light to the heart of your friend. As the wheel of truth begins to turn, let them receive the blessing of the truth. Let them feel held by the loving energy of your heart's light. Do not let the wheel turn different colours, this is not necessary. Let your friend receive the white light of truth, the light that illumines and heals.

When you are ready, let the wheel contract to the grail in your heart, as you bring back the ray you sent to your friend. Let the grail contract to a jewel, and let this diamond rest in your heart. Thank the ray and its angels for their blessing.

SHARING THIS RING IN A GROUP

The blessing of this ray can be shared in a larger group, but only stage one and two. It can be useful for groups of people who are feeling disillusioned and confused, having lost faith in everything.

It can also help those who have no direction, who have been misled. Through its reception they will feel the light of their own truth which offers them a point of reference, and a path to healing. Without a point of reference we easily get lost. If your point of reference is a light in your heart, you have found a guide that can lead you home.

Repeat the invocation and then let everyone in the group do stage one. Continue to stage two. Let everyone bring down the diamond above their heads and let it fall into the chalice in their heart. Let everyone form a wheel of truth around themselves. Then let all the little wheels merge into one big wheel that encircles the group. Let spokes of light from the big wheel connect to every heart, and then let everyone fill the wheel with light from the overflowing chalice within. Together let them turn the wheel of truth. Then they can go on to experience the blessing of each of the rings, as they turn the great white wheel from crimson to purple, to indigo blue, to sapphire blue, to rose pink, to emerald green, to gold, to orange and then to white again.

Let the great wheel slow down. Let it contract to the chalice within, and then to the diamond in each one's heart. Let each group member feel the radiance of their own jewel, the point of their own truth. They can now find their way aided by the compass of the heart, guided by a reference point of light within.

Remember to thank the ray for its ring and for its angels.

The Window of Grace

THE WINDOW OF GRACE

The spirit in the centre of the innermost dome looks up through the open window of grace. It sees a cross burning in a fire. In the centre of the cross, whose arms are of equal length, is a transparent jewel. Around the fire are rings of flame. In the rings of flame sit the spirits of those who passed through this window before. The spirit knows that if it chooses to ascend, it will fly through the open window, into the fire of the cross. If it chooses to stay where it is, the round window will close. The spirit will remain for a while at the top of the uppermost dome, before descending to join the other spirits in one of the coloured rings below. Having realised the point of truth, its spiritual journey is complete. Having glimpsed the fire above it has been shown a deeper dimension of grace, a dimension that it did not choose to explore further.

A MOMENT OF RECOGNITION

If the spirit chooses to pass through the window, it will fly into the fire. It knows that there is no way it can come back once it has passed through. If it chooses to fly through it does so in a moment of recognition, overwhelmed with love. This moment comes as it sees that the other spirits sitting round the cross in rings of flame chose the fire out of love for their kind. The spirit would rather be where they are, choosing as they chose, than remain where it is. It follows them understanding why they chose the fire. They chose it in order to keep it turning, for the sake of the others below. The fire of the cross is the origin of the point of unity and its rings, the fire of friendship, and all illumination that leads to spiritual growth. If nobody chooses to turn this fire, then eventually it goes out.

RETURNING TO GRACE

The spirit makes its choice with full awareness of all that is involved. It understands how rising to turn the fire will complete its own journey, a journey back to grace. It knows that this fire is where it belongs, and that these are the spirits with whom it is most at home. The new arrival flies through the window and takes its place in the centre of the cross that is burning in the fire. Encircling the four arms of the cross is a ring of flame. Spreading out behind this ring are many other burning rings.

Everyone in and around the fire has their own place, and there is a dignity and order in this placement. The new spirit in the fire feels the welcome of all who sat in the centre before. It needs no outward welcome, but feels their inner welcome as it burns. As it burns it loses consciousness of itself, and its individual identity as one who lived in a certain place, in a certain time. It feels the kinship of the ages that goes beyond time.

THE SUBSTITUTE OF THE AGE

As it sits in the centre of the fire the new arrival feels a loving presence behind it. It feels hands placed on its shoulders supporting it as it begins to burn. The loving spirit behind it is the Substitute of the Age. The Substitute of the Age is the premier candle of the age, an age being two thousand years. All the friends are candles who have burned away their own being in the light of the truth. The premier candle is the strongest, brightest one, who illumines all the others. The Substitute of the Piscean Age (the last two thousand years) is Jesus. He is also the Substitute for the Aquarian Age, the new age. The being of Jesus is a perfect channel for the light of the Christ, the light of the jewel of the cross. Jesus holds the newcomer's shoulders and the new substitute is invested with the light of the Christ.

For the last two thousand years all those who reached this fire on their spiritual path, have been effaced in the Substitute of the Age, although many were not 'Christians' in a traditional sense. Mansur al Hallaj, of the Islamic faith, and others robed in the light of their own spiritual tradition, received the deepest level of grace through their effacement in the light of the substitution. In this way they illumined their time, with the same light that illumined the ages past, the light at the centre of the cross, the light of a timeless jewel. The names of individuals and of religions change, but the true light does not change. Grace does not change, and its jewel remains the same, a hidden treasure that illumines all time.

THE LIGHT OF THE ANCIENT MYSTERIES

All the great religions of the world took their light from this fire, as did the ancient mystery schools. In every true spiritual school of the past there was a hidden teaching for the most advanced. They were taught that the goal behind all spiritual growth and endeavour was not personal liberation, but self-sacrifice for love. Through illumined teaching they learned that sacrifice itself could be transcended, and that in this transcendence was true liberation. This was a hidden teaching because the majority of aspirants would not be able to understand it, or practice it. But through the understanding of the few who could, this fire was kept alight through the ages.

THE LEVEL OF BEING OF A SUBSTITUTE

Unless you understand this hidden teaching, you cannot evolve to the level of being required of a substitute. A substitute is an individual who gives themselves for the whole. They take the place of everyone else in the fire. By reaching this level of unconditional love and selflessness, they become a clear channel for truth. The true light then illumines them. This true light is the light of grace, the light at the centre of the cross that all the substitutes radiate. It is the same light that all of us possess within. But until you make a personal choice to live for the whole and not for yourself, you are not fully conscious of the true nature of your own light.

THE POINT OF GRACE IS FORGIVENESS

As it is effaced in the light of the Christ, the spirit understands that the jewel at the centre of the cross is a point of grace, a point of forgiveness. It understands that forgiveness is that which heals and makes whole creation, so that it may return to a state of grace, in which no forgiveness is necessary. It understands that the action of burning in the fire is an act of forgiveness, where the individual offers their individual identity, in order to contribute to the healing of the whole. It understands that this giving can only be true if it is a real choice, a choice that is motivated by unconditional love.

THE CHOICE TO FORGIVE

To make the choice to forgive is to leave behind the limited conception of yourself as a part, understanding that in truth we are the whole. As long as one of us is in pain, all of us are. As long as one of us is destructive and cruel, all of us are. Understanding its connection to the whole, the spirit chooses forgiveness, so that all of us can forgive, and chooses love, so that we may all choose love. It makes a choice for healing from a state of integrated wholeness. It is able to make this choice, to choose forgiveness and love, because it has been nurtured and led by the light of those who made this choice before. In this way true spiritual teaching and guidance helps us to evolve beyond our present level of understanding. We depend on the spiritual evolution of all who went before us, whose teaching helps us to be human, and whose spiritual direction leads us back to grace.

THE SYMBOL OF GRACE

As the spirit burns in the fire, it gives itself; as it does so, it understands that the symbol of grace is a turning cross. It sits in the centre of the fire, supported by the Substitute of the Age, and the cross beneath it begins to turn. As the cross turns, the spirit understands the turning point of grace translated in its symbol, the symbol it has made real. The turning point of grace is the jewel at the centre of the cross. This point is a point of uncreated light. As the cross turns this point feeds the fire.

The light of the fire ensures that a path to grace is illumined, it keeps open a path of return. By choosing to turn the cross, the spirit chooses to expand the illumination of grace that begins in a point. It chooses for motives of unconditional love. Through an individual choice, the whole is helped to return to grace. Without an individual choice, grace would not be real. The point of grace is that the spirit loves enough to keep the fire burning for everyone else, by turning its central point. They are motivated to do this because they have lost their selfishness, in identification with the whole. Through its choice to give itself for love, because it knows it is love, the substitute heals all splits of you and me, here and there, before and after, and makes grace real for all, in every time and place.

THE CREATIVITY OF GRACE

As the spirit turns the jewel at the centre of the cross, it under-stands how grace is creative. It understands how this turning point turns the point of unity (the point of truth), from which the dimensions of created being spring. For the substitute is still connected to the point of truth, through a transcendent thread. With the advent of a new substitute in the fire, the point of truth is turned as the spirit turns the cross, and this turning renews spiritual illumination within the domes, and beyond. In this sense the point of grace is universally creative, ensuring the continuance of created form and spiritual illumination.

A SUBSTITUTE FOR ADAM

Adam is the archetype of humanity, and until all of his children have returned to full consciousness, a substitute chooses to burn in the place of Adam, and turn the fire for all of his kind. In this way they ensure the continued temporal and spiritual order of the universe, by turning its original point. Their motive for turning the fire is unconditional love, and this is the same energy that shines through the jewel at the centre of the cross.

By finding this level of unconditional love within themselves, they unite the light of Adam with the light of the Christ. In truth they are the same light, that of uncreated grace. In reality we never fell from grace, we never could. We just forgot that buried within us is the jewel of the cross that first gave us light. Grace is made real, and expanded out in creative rings of expression, through the sacrifice of its substitutes, who understand its point. They have reached a level of being where grace is always alive, the point at the centre of the cross. They take Adam's place in the fire of the beginning, thereby keeping it alight and ensuring the continued spiritual evolution of all of his children.

THE ORDER OF THE CROSS

In the turning fire the spirit understands that they are burning for their brothers, so that their brothers may come to recognise who they truly are. For this service they receive the Order of the Cross, as a golden cross with a diamond at its centre is placed on a chain around their neck. They receive this honour in the right spirit, having left behind any desire to shine as an individual. They now shine as a link in a chain, that is held together by its central jewel, the Substitute of the Age.

The new substitute knows that they are a channel for the light of the Christ, the light that they truly are. They know that everyone alive is also a channel for this light, although they may not be conscious of this yet. They know that the cross on a chain that they now wear connects them to the whole, that their brother's life is their life. Thus they receive the cross in a spirit of humility and gratitude, knowing that it is given to them to share. The Order of the Cross is the spiritual rank of the substitutes, those who choose to burn in Adam's place and share the blessing of his true light.

As the spirit receives this order, the cross on which it sits begins to turn more quickly, turning the inner ring of the cross. From this motion the outer rings of flame begin to turn also. As the turning of the rings of flame accelerates, the cross on which the fire rests turns faster and faster.

THE UNIVERSAL TURNING OF THE CROSS

The cross of flame within a burning circle now begins to turn around, and its turning is in all directions, not just a horizontal turning, but also a vertical, and diagonal turning. As the cross turns in all directions the spirit loses awareness of itself, and begins to assimilate an understanding of universal grace. Grace is universal for it is the origin of the universe, but it is also universal because it turns in all directions. Thus, whichever way we go, sooner or later we turn to grace. In other words, the universe is itself an expression of grace, for grace is its essence, its origin, and the point of its return.

Everything created is returning to grace in its own way, and this return to grace is understood by the turning spirit in musical terms, as a harmonious symphony being played out through the instrument of matter. Grace returns to itself through all the highs and lows of human existence, and through the cacophony of conflict on earth. Try as we might, we cannot lose the golden thread of original grace, even if we can no longer recognise it. The spirit understands that all things begin and end in grace, and that all universes always did and always will.

THE CALL OF UNIVERSAL GRACE

A return to perfect wholeness is a return to grace without beginning or end. By now, through the action of its turning, the cross and circle around it have become a spinning ball of flame.

Within this ball of flame the new substitute begins to breathe with the breath of universal grace. As it breathes it starts to call. In its calling song the spirit affirms the existence of the uncreated light of grace, bearing witness to it through its own burning.

The spirit feels the ball of fire slowing down, and the circles around it becoming visible. The thread of transcendent flame that links the spirit to the fire of friendship below has remained connected to the spirit all this time. As the cross slows down it continues to turn in graceful revolutions, in all directions. The spirit has initiated the multi-dimensional turning of the cross within the fire.

THE EFFECT OF THE TURNING OF THE CROSS

The spirit that sits in the centre of the cross that turns in all directions looks down to the domes below. The thread of flame that connects the spirit to the point of truth, and the fire of friendship, is turning at great speed like a maypole.

The turning of the point of truth and the fire of friendship causes the rings of grace to turn more swiftly. This acceleration produces a great outpouring of light, which falls through the windows in the domes, and through the open window of friendship, down to the levels below. The spirit in the fire sees that the universal turning of the cross has illumined the path of return. It sees that the turning of the domes and the turning of the fire of the friends has illumined all the windows below, and brought the light of grace down to the lowest stairs. As a torrent of light reaches the bottom of the tower, the door of faith is flung open by the force of the light, so that many now find their way to an open door that leads them home.

A SYMBOL OF BLESSING

The substitutes are those who see through all illusion, to the point of grace. As they turn the universal cross of grace, they see through their own sacrifice. Grace is the point that is loving and forgiving, as is the substitute who accepts the cross. All who turned the cross before, and all who will in future, understand the true nature of forgiveness, the point of original grace. Becoming this point, they affirm the uncreated nature of grace, which is beyond the beginning and end of all things. Seeing through the cross, the substitute understands why it had to make a choice, why it had to be a volunteer. Their choice proved their unconditional love. Once proven they realise that in truth there is no sacrifice, there is nothing but grace. All else is recognised as illusory and transient. As they see through the cross it ceases to be a symbol of sacrifice, and becomes a symbol of blessing.

THE ANTHEM OF THE AGE

As the new substitute sees through their own sacrifice, the window of grace slowly closes, so that the spirit can no longer see the domes, or the fire of friendship below. It continues its call, and the rings around the fire reverberate with sound, as the other substitutes echo the new substitute's song. Each age has its own song, the song that illumines their portion of the universal calendar. At the end of an age the song of the inner circle combines, as the notes of each century are present. As the new substitute sings the inner wheel turns, and the future is born, in harmony and grace. The new comer is overwhelmed by the beauty of the turning zodiac, as the anthem of past ages echoes with its own.

THE SONG OF THE FUTURE

If there were no more substitutes the future would lose its song, as it lost its light. They would both fade away together. This does not happen until the end of a particular universal cycle, when the Divine breath returns to itself. Then the cycles of time, space and matter contract to the point of unity, which returns to the point of grace. The cross and the rings of flame around it also contract to this point as the fire dies down. All that is left at the end of a universal cycle is a timeless point of grace, a hidden treasure that contains all within itself. As this point breathes out, a new cycle is born, as from this point all unfolds again.

HIDDEN LINKS IN A CHAIN OF GRACE

This is why there are always volunteers who choose to turn the fire, substitutes for each generation, until the appointed end of a universal cycle. Most of these are people who led unremarkable outer lives, individuals unknown to history. Hidden links in a chain of grace, they never wanted or received any kind of recognition for their lives of service. The new substitute recognises its debt to all of those who burned before, to those loving selfless souls who sang in turn, that we might have a future.

The new substitute knows that everything unfolds according to the Divine plan, and that there is an awe-inspiring order and harmony in the precise working out of this plan. The new substitute feels the awe of all who taste the power of the Divine Breath, the Breath that turns the universal cycle in a dance of pre-destined grace. The newcomer has no fear of this Breath. It has surrendered its destiny to love, and it knows that behind the might and power of the universe is a jewel of pure merciful grace.

THE SONG OF BLESSING

The newcomer has to be living in a material body when they make their choice for the fire, and thereby become a substitute. If everything happened in the higher realms, the song would not materialise. The substitution happens when they are living in a body, for then they can bring the song of heaven down to earth, as they affirm the unity of grace. This affirmation they make as they sing the song of reparation, the song of blessing that forgives all evil and makes all well. This song of blessing returns all things to grace, in which there is no sacrifice. The new arrival sings this song as they turn the fire, while still living as a human being on earth.

OUR TRUE SONG

The return to grace is a return to a state of being that we essentially are. The song of blessing is our song, the song that unites us, and gives us a future. Having completed the journey of self-knowledge, the individual discovers that their struggle, their choices, and their sacrifice, were the lessons whereby they learned to sing their true song. Grace is forgiving ourselves and others for not being perfectly loving, perfectly well, and perfectly whole. Through this forgiveness we affirm the unity of grace, the harmony that we were at the beginning, that we are again at the end. This remains our song whichever level we are on. We discover it through our journey, a journey of return, return to faith, return to love, return to grace.

THE RAY OF GRACE

Rays from the fire of grace descend through the rose window of grace into the domes below. From here the rays filter through the window of friendship, which is directly beneath the window of grace, at the bottom of the domes. From the window of friendship coloured rays of grace fall down to earth.

You feel the influence of a ray of grace at times in your life when you are befriended by the Divine. Such an experience fills your heart with love and peace. It is a feeling of deep friendship, as your spirit is held in the embrace of unconditional love. This experience can happen to anyone, anywhere. Such touches of grace, which are rare, give you certain proof that a realm beyond the physical exists, and that you are personally cared about by a universal power. After having had such an experience people often actively seek a spiritual path.

A RAY OF GRACE THROUGH THE DOORWAY OF A FRIEND

A less dramatic experience of grace can happen when you receive the light of grace through the doorway of an illumined friend. The rays of grace that shine through a true friend of grace will always bring you comfort, illumination and understanding. One way that anyone can receive a glimmer of these rays is to read the books that friends left behind for us. Four pieces of writing, through which you can receive the energy of grace, are:

The Sermon on the Mount - Jesus' words in Mathew 5:1-16
The Fire of Love - by Richard Rolle
Revelations of Divine Love - by Julian of Norwich
The Mathnawi - by Jalalu'ddin Rumi

Through their written words these friends of grace can assist you on a path of patience, humility and love. If you find their books difficult to read, do not worry. If you can't receive their blessing through their books, ask for it directly. The help of the friends is always available if you ask for it with sincere need. A few others who can be relied on to give you good counsel (although there are many more) are: John of the Cross, Francis of Assisi, Teresa of Avila, Hildegard of Bingen, and Mansur-al-Hallaj. You can also ask for help from friends who lived closer to our own time such as Dr Edward Bach and Father Bede Griffiths.

Do not be shy to ask for help, just because you feel that these individuals lived a long time ago, and may have followed a path very different to yours. True friends of grace will never judge you. They no longer live in time. In the timeless realm they exist to help at every level, to help you progress on your path. True friends have understood the point of forgiveness, and cannot treat you without love.

THE ANGELS OF GRACE

The angels of grace bring the light of graceful understanding. This is the understanding that sees everything in terms of the infinite gracefulness of the whole. The angels of grace appear robed in flame to touch the lives of those who are ready to be servants of the Divine plan. These angels help people see their role of service within it. They are messengers reminding Adam's children of their original light, and helping them to share this light through illumined revelation and transmission.

The angels of grace touch with flame the spirits of those whose aspiration is noble and pure. They befriend all those who long for God with sincere need. They come to those who wish to dedicate their lives to truth, and they inspire them with a breath of fire.

THE RECEPTION OF THE RAY OF GRACE

You can receive the touch of a ray of grace, if you ask for it with sincerity, and open yourself to receive it.

Follow the instructions at the end of the book for grounding and centring the body.

Imagine a rose window about a foot above your head. This window is inlaid with precious stones, rubies, sapphires, emeralds, amethysts and diamonds. As you focus on it say:

> " May I receive the blessing of a ray of grace.
> May the angels of grace please be with me."

Feel different coloured rays of light falling down on your head from the window above. Feel these rays enveloping your outer body in a shower of light. You may feel the hands of an angel of flame holding your shoulders, holding you tenderly. Your back and shoulders may feel warm, as you sense their touch.

Let this rain of coloured light align your inner and outer bodies. When all our bodies (physical, etheric, emotional, and mental) are aligned we feel well balanced, healthy, and radiant. Let the rays of grace bring your bodies into alignment, the alignment of grace. Let them smooth out any knots in your inner and outer being. Feel yourself becoming smooth, light and gracefully aligned.

Then let the window above you slowly open. Look up and see a burning cross in a ring of flame. From the jewel at the centre of this cross let a ray of flame descend from the fire to the crown of your head. Let it enter your body here, and then take this ray down your spine and out into the earth beneath you. Then bring it back up your spine, and let it come to rest in your heart centre. There let this ray of flame crystallise into a transparent jewel. From this diamond let four golden arms extend horizontally, so that this jewel becomes the central stone in an equal armed cross. In your heart you now hold a golden cross with a diamond at its centre.

Know that the light of this diamond exists to forgive all harm, to burn away all that is other than love. As you find your own jewel, let go of all that is other than love within you. Allow yourself to feel the pure love that you are. Forgive all of you that is less than loving. Forgive everyone else as well. Forgive yourself in the knowledge that this stone of grace can show you who you truly are. It knows your true beauty; it knows your perfect grace. It knows that all else that you believed to be true was an illusion, a dream from which you are awakening.

In forgiveness find your key, the key that turns the cross. As your cross starts to turn around, look within and allow yourself to see your true face. Allow yourself to see yourself as you truly are, not as you would like to be, but as you truly, essentially are. Let go of the illusion of yourself as other than loving and forgiving. In essence we are full of grace. As you learn to forgive, you turn to grace. As the cross turns horizontally let it trace a golden circle around your heart.

Gradually let the cross in your heart slow down and become still. Let the four arms of the golden cross contract to their central stone. Hold this jewel in your heart. Let the window above you close, and as it does so say:

"I thank the ray of grace for the jewel of the cross."

Make sure you are well grounded and centred before you open your eyes.

THE DEEPER RECEPTION OF THE RAY OF GRACE
If you would like to receive the deeper blessing of this light, you can ask for it. Do stage one, then say:

"May I receive the deeper blessing of the ray of grace.
May I feel the blessing of its ring."

Expand the four arms of the cross horizontally so that they extend to two feet beyond your body. Let them slowly begin to turn. As they do let them create a circle of light two feet around your body. You are now encircled by a ring of light, turned by an equal armed cross of gold. The centre stone of the cross remains in your heart. As the cross and its ring turns, repeat the word 'Grace'. Rest in the radiance of your own grace.

After a while, turn your attention to the window above your head that is still open. On the other side of it see again the cross burning in a fire, surrounded by rings of flame. Slowly bring this cross and its surrounding ring of flame down to meet the cross within you. Bring it down on a ray of flame. Let the cross and the ring of fire above expand as they descend, so that they can merge with the ring that encircles you. Bring down the upper cross right through your body, to meet its counterpart, so that the central jewel of the cross above meets and merges with the jewel in your heart. Let the ring of fire from above gently meet the ring of light around you, as the two crosses unite.

Now let the golden cross within you turn more quickly. As the cross turns faster let the diamond at its centre burst into flames. Feel the fire created in your heart, by the motion of a swiftly turning jewel. In this fire is your starting point, the jewel of your own grace.

Know that this point of grace is the centre of you, and that you never ended or began. Feel the security of your divinity, the security of your essential spark. And through this security, forgive yourself for doubting that this point of grace is the truth in you. Rest in the radiance of your essence, in the centre of your creative fire. Rest here for as long as you want, breathing in the fire of your uncreated grace.

Let the burning cross slow down and come to a standstill. Now bring in the flames of the burning ring around you; let them contract into the central point of grace, the diamond at the centre of the cross. Then let the four arms of the cross also contract into this central point. Feel the jewel in the centre of your heart. Within this jewel you contain the cross of grace and its fire. Become like a candle and live in remembrance of this jewel, as your life becomes a journey into grace. Let the window above you close as you say:

" *I thank the ray of grace for the blessing of its ring.*"

Ground yourself fully before you open your eyes.

THE DEEPEST RECEPTION OF THE RAY OF GRACE
If you would like to receive the deepest reception of this ray you can. This reception is not difficult to do, if you trust that it can be done. Allow it to happen, and it will happen easily. It is the culmination of all the receptions, the crown of them all.

Go through stage one and two, and rest in the centre of a burning cross, encircled by a ring of flame. Then say:

"May I receive the deepest blessing of the ray of grace.
May I receive the blessing of the substitution."

Let the burning cross begin to turn, and as it does so, let it turn in all directions, not just around you, but up and down, and diagonally. Let it rotate in a universal movement from its central stone. As it turns in all directions, let the circle of light around you become a spinning ball of flame. You are at the centre of a cross that turns in all direction, encircled by a ball of flame. Then let the cross gradually slow down.

You are still surrounded by a ball of flame, created by the

turning of the cross and its ring. Within this ball of flame become aware of a presence behind you. Become aware of one behind you who holds your shoulders, one whose loving face wears a crown of thorns. Let yourself feel the support of Jesus, the Substitute of the Age, as he offers you the blessing of your own light, the light of the Christ.

Take this blessing. Receive from Jesus the light of the Christ, the light of uncreated grace. This is also your light, because it is Adam's light, it belongs to humankind. It is the jewel of the cross, hidden in our clay, the jewel of our divinity. You cannot find it without love. As you accept it, lose your face in the face behind you. Lose your self in his light. In so doing you will lose yourself in the light of the Christ, the light of your uncreated essence. The light of Adam and Christ unite in you as you receive the blessing of the substitution.

From now on at any time in your life you can ask Christ to be there instead of you. If you are working in service, healing or teaching, you can ask Christ to be there in your place. In truth all of us are the Christ, and all of us together make up the fullness of the Christ. Our personalities prevent us from seeing this truth, and living in full awareness of our own Christhood, and our unity with all life. I am not suggesting you somehow lose your personality and pretend to be Christ. I suggest you allow yourself consciously to become a channel for the Christ light, as at certain times you offer yourself as a substitute for grace.

In your meditations, or in any work where compassion is required, allow your true Christ-like self to be there, instead of the you that is less than true. By asking Christ to be with you, you are not really asking someone else to be there. You are asking your own true light to shine through the layers you have laid upon it. You are asking your own jewel to reveal itself. If you ask with simple faith, the substitution is easy. You just show who you truly are.

Feel the strength of this perfectly graceful blessing as you slowly contract the cross and its ring to the jewel in your heart. Look up at the open window above you, and as it closes say:

"I thank the ray of grace for the blessing of the substitution."

Make sure you are well grounded and centred before you open your eyes.

You can remember this blessing at any time of the day, until it becomes second nature. As it does you will effortlessly return to grace.

CONCLUSION

Now at the end of the present age, humanity has advanced enough to seek a path to grace en masse, not just in cloistered monasteries, or in schools of esoteric learning. Many people want to begin a spiritual path in earnest, they want to unlock their inner treasury and discover their true wealth. All of us are born to return to grace. All of us have a means of access; all of us have a jewel of light within that can lead us home. Nobody is excluded. Grace is for all of us, it is our inheritance. The rays of grace are accessible to all. They descend to bring us faith, hope and love, and to help us find our way home.

Open your inner treasury with humility and gratitude. Receive your inheritance in the right spirit. Let the wealth of grace that you discover give you more to share. Do not waste the jewel of the cross, the treasure of your own essential grace. Be grateful for the rays of grace and share them with a sincere heart, as you learn to let Christ live in your place. Make your heart the rose window that hides a fire, a silver grail, a golden cross and a jewel of grace. For your heart is where you will share with others the wealth of your inheritance, the inheritance of the new age. And your heart is where you begin your journey, an old, old journey, the same in every age, the journey of all of Adam's children back to grace.

APPENDICES

A TREASURY OF GRACE

SUMMARY OF THE RAYS OF GRACE :
THEIR INVOCATIONS, WORDS AND SYMBOLS

THE ORANGE RAY OF TRANSCENDENCE
For those who are confused, unable to move forward.

Reception of the Ray of Transcendence
> *"May I receive the grace of the orange ray of transcendence.*
> *May the angels of transcendence please be with me."*

> *" I thank the ray of transcendence for the pillar of its grace."*

SYMBOL: PILLAR OF FLAME

The Deeper Reception of the Ray of Transcendence
"May I receive the deeper grace of the orange ray of transcendence.
> *May I feel the blessing of its ring."*

> *"I thank the ray of transcendence for the blessing of its ring."*

SYMBOL: THE RING OF TRANSCENDENCE
WORD: JOY

THE GOLD RAY OF ILLUMINATION
For those who are in despair.
Especially for those who are suicidal, who need hope.

Reception of the Ray of Illumined Grace
> *"May I receive the grace of the golden ray of illumination.*
> *May the angels of illumination please be with me."*

> *" I thank the ray of illumination for the candle of its grace."*

SYMBOL: CANDLE

The Deeper Reception of the Ray of Illumined Grace
"May I receive the deeper grace of the golden ray of illumination.
> *May I feel the blessing of its ring."*

> *"I thank the ray of illumination for the blessing of its ring."*

SYMBOL: THE RING OF PROTECTION
WORD: LIGHT

Sharing this Ring with Others
"May we receive the deeper grace of the golden ray of illumination.
May we feel the blessing of its ring.
May the angels of illumination please be with us."

THE EMERALD RAY OF UNIFIED LIFE
For those who are exhausted and out of balance.

Reception of the Ray of Unified Life
"May I receive the grace of the emerald ray of life.
May the angels of life please be with me."

"I thank the ray of life for the fountain of its grace."

SYMBOL: FOUNTAIN

The Deeper Reception of the Ray of Unified Life
"May I receive the deeper grace of the emerald ray of life.
May I feel the blessing of its ring."

"I thank the ray of life for the blessing of its ring."

SYMBOL: THE RING OF LIFE
WORD: HARMONY

Sharing this Ring with Others
"May we receive the deeper grace of the emerald ray of life.
May we feel the blessing of its ring.
May the angels of life please be with us."

THE ROSE PINK RAY OF ABUNDANT BLESSING
For those who are empty, who have nothing to give.
Especially for those recovering from addiction, who need
spiritual nourishment.

The Reception of the Ray of Abundant Blessing
"May I receive the grace of the rose pink ray of abundant blessing.
May the angels of blessing please be with me."

"I thank the ray of blessing for the rain of its grace."

SYMBOL: OPEN TREASURE CHEST

The Deeper Reception of the Ray of Abundant Blessing
"May I receive the deeper grace of the rose pink ray
of abundant blessing.
May I feel the blessing of its ring."

"I thank the ray of abundant blessing for the blessing of its ring."

SYMBOL: THE WHEEL OF BLESSING
WORD: BLESSING

Sharing this Ring with Others
"May we receive the deeper grace of the rose pink ray
of abundant blessing.
May we feel the blessing of its ring.
May the angels of blessing please be with us."

THE SAPPHIRE RAY OF COMPASSIONATE PEACE
For those who are weary and anxious, who need support.
Especially for victims of abuse.

Reception of the Ray of Compassionate Peace
"May I receive the blessing of the sapphire ray
of compassionate peace.
May the angels of compassion please be with me."

"I thank the ray of compassionate peace for the tears of its grace."

SYMBOL: A TEAR

The Deeper Reception of the Ray of Compassionate Peace
"May I receive the deeper grace of the sapphire ray of compassionate peace.
May I feel the blessing of its ring."

"I thank the ray of compassionate peace for the blessing of its ring."

SYMBOL: THE WHEEL OF PEACE
WORD: PEACE

Sharing this Ring with Others
"May we receive the deeper grace of the ray of compassionate peace.
May we feel the blessing of its ring.
May the angels of compassion please be with us."

THE INDIGO RAY OF SACRED HEALING
For those who are sick in mind, body and spirit.
Especially for those who cannot trust themselves.

Reception of the Ray of Sacred Healing
" May I receive the grace of the indigo ray of sacred healing.
May the angels of healing please be with me."

"I thank the ray of sacred healing for the staff of its grace."

SYMBOL: A GOLD STAFF

The Deeper Reception of the Ray of Sacred Healing
" May I receive the deeper grace of the ray of sacred healing.
May I feel the blessing of its ring."

"I thank the ray of sacred healing for the blessing of its ring."

SYMBOL: THE WHEEL OF HEALING
WORD: TRUST

Sharing this Ring with Others
"May we receive the deeper grace of the indigo ray of sacred healing.

May we feel the blessing of its ring.
May the angels of healing please be with us."

THE PURPLE RAY OF ETERNITY
For those who fear change.
Especially for those who are terminally ill.

Reception of the Ray of Eternity
"May I receive the grace of the purple ray of eternity.
May the angels of eternity please be with me."

" I thank the ray of eternity for the ring of its grace."

SYMBOL: A SILVER RING

The Deeper Reception of the Ray of Eternity
"May I receive the deeper grace of the purple ray of eternity.
May I feel the blessing of its ring."

"I thank the ray of eternity for the blessing of its ring."

SYMBOL: THE WHEEL OF ETERNITY
WORD: RETURN

The Deepest Reception of the Ray of Eternity
" May I receive the deepest blessing of the ray of eternity.
May I receive the communion of the ring."

"I thank the ray of eternity for the communion of the ring."

SYMBOL: THE CALL OF THE RING
PHRASE: ETERNAL LIFE

Sharing this Ring with Others
" May we receive the deeper blessing of the ray of eternity.
May we receive the blessing of its ring.
May the angels of eternity please be with us."

THE CRIMSON RAY OF DIVINE LOVE
For those who are afraid to love.
Especially for those who cannot trust others.

Reception of the Ray of Divine Love
"May I receive the grace of the crimson ray of divine love.
May the angels of love please be with me."

"I thank the ray of divine love for the rose of its grace."

SYMBOL: A CRIMSON ROSE

The Deeper Reception of the Ray of Divine Love
" May I receive the deeper grace of the crimson ray of divine love.
May I feel the blessing of its ring."

"I thank the ray of divine love for the blessing of its ring."

SYMBOL: THE WHEEL OF DIVINE LOVE
WORD: LOVE

The Deepest Reception of the Ray of Divine Love
"May I receive the deepest blessing of the crimson ring of divine love.
May I receive the communion of the rose."

" I thank the crimson ray of divine love for the communion of the rose."

SYMBOL: THE REVOLUTION OF THE WHEEL OF DIVINE LOVE
PHRASE: NOTHING BUT LOVE

Sharing this Ring with Others
"May we receive the grace of the crimson ray of divine love.
May we feel the blessing of its ring.
May the angels of love please be with us."

THE WHITE RAY OF TRUTH
For those who are lost, who need clarity and direction.
Especially for those who have been misled.

Reception of the Ray of Truth:
"May I receive the grace of the white ray of truth.
May the angels of truth please be with me."

"I thank the ray of truth for the grail of its grace."

SYMBOL: A SILVER GRAIL

The Deeper Reception of the Ray of Truth:
"May I receive the deeper grace of the white ray of truth.
May I feel the blessing of its ring."

"I thank the ray of truth for the blessing of its ring."

SYMBOL: THE WHEEL OF TRUTH
WORD: TRUTH

The Deepest Reception of the Ray of Truth:
"May I receive the deepest blessing of the ray of truth.
May I receive the communion of the grail."

"I thank the ray of truth for the communion of the grail."

SYMBOL: A POINT
PHRASE: THE POINT OF TRUTH IS WITHIN ME

Sharing this Ring with Others
"May we feel the deeper blessing of the white ray of truth.
May we feel the blessing of its ring.
May the angels of truth please be with us."

THE RAY OF GRACE
For Everyone

Reception of the Ray of Grace
>*"May I receive the blessing of a ray of grace.*
>*May the angels of grace please be with me."*

>*"I thank the ray of grace for the jewel of the cross"*

SYMBOL: A GOLD CROSS WITH A DIAMOND AT ITS CENTRE

The Deeper Reception of the Ray of Grace
>*"May I receive the deeper blessing of the ray of grace.*
>*May I feel the blessing of its ring."*

>*"I thank the ray of grace for the blessing of its ring."*

SYMBOL: A BURNING CROSS IN A RING OF FIRE
WORD: GRACE

The Deepest Reception of the Ray of Grace
>*"May I receive the deepest blessing of the ray of grace.*
>*May I receive the blessing of the substitution."*

>*" I thank the ray of grace for the blessing of the substitution."*

SYMBOL: THE CHRIST
PHRASE: CHRIST BE WITH ME

INSTRUCTIONS FOR RECEIVING THE RAYS OF GRACE

INSTRUCTIONS FOR GROUNDING AND CENTRING THE BODY TO BE DONE BEFORE THE RECEPTION OF THE RAYS OF GRACE

1. Sit comfortably on a chair or on the floor. Allow your body and mind to relax. If it helps you to relax, you can imagine yourself in a favourite place in the natural world, somewhere beautiful and peaceful.

2. Become aware of your breathing. Allow your body to relax more deeply as you breathe more deeply.

3. Imagine two roots coming out of the soles of your feet and going deep into the earth, connecting you to the centre of the earth. Imagine a large taproot descending from the base of your spine, to connect with the centre of the earth.

4. Imagine the energy of the earth coming up your 'roots' and holding you firmly. Feel a deep sense of connection to the ground. Feel the heartbeat of the earth beneath you; let yourself breathe with the earth. Let your breath flow down your roots, into the earth.

5. Bring the earth's energy up your feet, legs and abdomen. Then focus on your centre, your navel. Focus on a warm ball of light at your navel. Breathe into this point. Feel the stability of your centre.

6. Be aware of what it is like to feel relaxed, grounded and centred. Be aware of this feeling, so that at the end of the meditation you can ground and centre yourself again if you need to.

THE NOURISHMENT OF THE RAYS OF GRACE

The lights of grace descend so that we may receive spiritual nourishment, nourishment of heart and spirit. Because you may not be used to it, it is best to build up your reception of the lights of grace gradually. The exercises to help you receive the rays are presented in three stages. It is better to become familiar with the first stage before proceeding to stage two. Stage two involves a deeper reception of each rays light, through receiving the blessing of its ring. The rays that issue from the innermost dome have a third stage to their reception. This stage is for those who are comfortable with stage one and two, and who would like to receive the communion of the rings of grace.

If you practice the reception of the rays of grace regularly, you will become accustomed to this kind of nourishment. You will notice the effect of your new spiritual 'diet' in your outer life. Your energy will change. The rays of grace will help you become spiritually pure and strong. They will help you to recognise your real self, to shed the false and find the true.

SHARING THE RAYS OF GRACE WITH ANOTHER PERSON OR IN A GROUP

I have given instructions on how to share some of the rays of grace with another person, or with a group who would benefit from their light. If sharing the rings in a group make sure everyone practices receiving a ray on their own, before attempting the group reception. Also at least one person in the group should be familiar with the reception of all the rays at all their stages, and know the instructions in detail. They can then explain to the rest of the group how to receive the rays during the group reception.

When members of the group are experienced at receiving the rays both individually and in a group, they can then go on to share the rays with a new group of people if they want to. Everyone who has felt the blessing of a ray is qualified to go on and share this blessing with others. Only two things are required, once you are familiar with the receptions. They are that you encourage an attitude of sincerity, reverence and gratitude during the reception of the rays, and that you do not charge any money for sharing their blessing in a group. Grace is free, and it is for everyone.

RECEIVING THE RAYS OF GRACE IN THE RIGHT SPIRIT

It is best to ask for the rays of grace in a reverent spirit, for this is how their blessing is best received. The spiritual influence of the rays and their angels respond to sincerity of intention and purity of motive. These will evoke their response. If you ask for them with greed, in hope of material or spiritual reward, you will block their way. You will be asking in the spirit of greed that always wants more because it fears that there is not enough. If you don't know how to ask in a reverent spirit, before you ask any of the rays to descend, follow these three simple steps:

1. Have a shower, or wash, and put on some clean clothes.
2. Say a short prayer, before you repeat the invocation. It can either be one that you know, or one that you make up. Say it with sincerity.
3. When you ask for the ray to descend, include the following sentence in the invocation:

*" May I receive the blessing of this ray with
reverence and gratitude."*

If you follow these simple steps with sincerity your request will be in the right spirit.

IF YOU ARE HAVING DIFFICULTY RECEIVING THE RAYS OF GRACE

If you experience difficulty in receiving the spiritual influence of the rays of grace, this may be because you are not asking for them with sincerity. You may not believe that the rays or their angels exist, and this may mean that you ask for them without any sincere intention. However you may still need their healing blessing.

Alternatively you may worry because you don't feel or see any angels, colours or anything else. You may find it hard to follow the instructions, and then convince yourself that you are not able to receive them. If you have caused others a lot of pain, you may fear that you are beyond forgiveness, and beyond the blessing of the rays of grace. If any of the above examples apply to you, then use this simple formula to ask for the rays:

*"Ray of illumination / unified life / compassionate peace / etc.,
if you are there please fall on me.
Angels of illumination, life, compassion etc.,
if you can hear me, please be with me.
Although I may not have faith in you / be good enough / be able
to forgive myself / my need is sincere."*

After some time you will be able to drop the above invocation. As you benefit from their blessing, you will begin to have faith in the ability of the rays and their angels to help you heal.

If you have trouble remembering the instructions for the receptions, this does not mean that you are not as 'spiritual' as someone who is able to follow them easily. It just means that your own way of receiving the rays may be better for you than any other way. The way I offer may suit some people, but others will need to find their own way. There is no right or wrong way to receive them. So do not be discouraged if you find my suggestions hard to follow. Just repeat the invocations, focus on the ray and its particular colour, and see it shining down on you from a ring above your head. You will receive the benefit of each ray as it descends. You do not actively have to do anything, except ask and receive.

You can find your own way to receive the rays of grace, for they are here for us all. You will receive the healing of the rays, if you ask with sincerity, for no one who comes hungry to this table is ever turned away. It is a treasury of grace for all us, the treasury of the new age.

EXPANDED TABLE OF CONTENTS

FOR INFORMATION ON

JOURNEY INTO GRACE

WORKSHOP GROUPS

CALL:

(LONDON) 0181 788 3092

www.ringofgrace.com
email: caroline@ringofgrace.com